Britain and the Suez Crisis

Making Contemporary Britain

General Editor: Anthony Seldon
Consultant Editor: Peter Hennessy

Published

Northern Ireland since 1968
Paul Arthur and Keith Jeffery

Britain and the Suez Crisis
David Carlton

British Defence since 1945
Michael Dockrill

Britain and the Falklands War
Lawrence Freedman

Forthcoming

British Industry since 1945
Margaret Ackrill

British General Elections since 1945
David Butler

Electoral Change since 1945
Ivor Crewe

The End of Empire
John Darwin

The Attlee Government
Peter Hennessy

Political Consensus since 1945
Dennis Kavanagh and Peter Morris

Crime and Criminal Justice since 1945
Terence Morris

The Mass Media
Colin Seymour-Ure

Government and the Unions
Robert Taylor

Terrorism
Paul Wilkinson

Institute of Contemporary British History
34 Tavistock Square, London WC1H 9EZ

Britain and the Suez Crisis

David Carlton

Basil Blackwell

First published 1988
First published in USA 1989

Basil Blackwell Ltd
108 Cowley Road, Oxford, OX4 1JF, UK

Basil Blackwell Inc.
432 Park Avenue South, Suite 1503
New York, NY 10016, USA

British Library Cataloguing in Publication Data
Carlton, David, *1938–*
    Britain and the Suez crisis. – (Making
    contemporary Britain).
    1. Suez crisis. Role of Great Britain
    I. Title   II. Series
    956´.044
    ISBN 0-631-16089-2
    ISBN 0-631-16091-4 Pbk

Library of Congress Cataloging in Publication Data
Carlton, David, 1938–
    Britain and the Suez crisis/David Carlton.
        p.   cm. – (Making contemporary Britain)
    Includes index.
    ISBN 0-631-16089-2   ISBN 0-631-16091-4 (pbk.)
    1. Egypt – History – Intervention, 1956.   2. Great Britain – Foreign
relations – 1945–   I. Title.   II. Series.
DT107.83.C37   1989
327.41062-dc19

                                                        88-19403
                                                        CIP

Typeset in 11 on 13 pt Ehrhardt
by Joshua Associates Ltd., Oxford
Printed in Great Britain by
Page Bros Ltd, Norwich

Contents

The Middle East

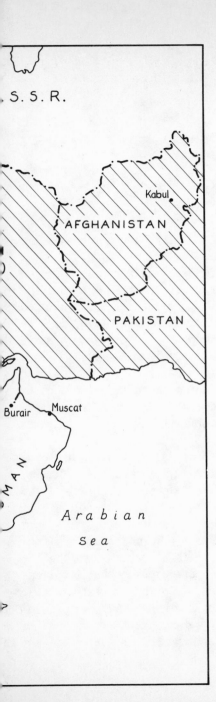

U. S. S. R.

Kabul

AFGHANISTAN

PAKISTAN

Burair · Muscat

OMAN

Arabian Sea

‖‖‖‖‖ Suez Canal

◩ Baghdad Pact

General Editor's Preface

The Institute of Contemporary British History's series *Making Contemporary Britain* is aimed at undergraduates, school students and others interested in learning more about topics in post-war British history. In the series, authors are attempting less to break new ground than to present clear and balanced overviews of the state of knowledge on each of the topics.

The ICBH was founded in October 1986 with the objective of promoting at every level the study of British history since 1945. To that end it publishes books and a quarterly journal, *Contemporary Record*; it organizes seminars and conferences for sixth-formers, undergraduates, researchers and teachers of post-war history; and it runs a number of research programmes and other activities.

A central belief in the ICBH's work is that post-war history is too often neglected in schools, institutes of higher education and beyond. The ICBH acknowledges the validity of the arguments against the study of recent history, notably the problems of bias, of overly subjective teaching and writing, and the difficulties of perspective. But it believes that the values of studying post-war history outweigh the drawbacks, and that the health and future of a liberal democracy require that its citizens know more about the most recent past of their country than the limited knowledge possessed by British citizens, young and old, today. Indeed, the ICBH believes that the dangers of political indoctrination are higher where the young are *not* informed of the recent past.

No event in the post-war period has so divided the nation as the Suez Crisis; in none has the government so adamantly obscured the truth, and there has been much controversy as to its effect on Britain's standing in the world. In consequence, many will see 1956 as one of the turning points in Britain's post-war history.

David Carlton is eminently qualified to write a book on the Suez Crisis. His highly praised biography of Anthony Eden and his writings in international history have equipped him well to understand the nuances of this tangled episode in recent British history.

In keeping with other volumes in the series, the book is comparatively short, and space considerations therefore precluded the presentation of much material recently released at the Public Record Office under the 30-year rule. Nevertheless, the author has attempted to take full account of the most important documents now available, and he has reproduced some of them in the Appendices so that readers may form their own judgements on some of the more contentious aspects.

Also, in keeping with the series, the author focuses on *British* history, examining the episode primarily from a British perspective. He is well aware that these events may appear very different when viewed from another national vantage point.

Anthony Seldon

Acknowledgements

I am indebted to Dr Anthony Seldon of the Institute of Contemporary British History and to Sean Magee of Basil Blackwell for advice and encouragement during the preparation of this volume. For typing, my thanks are due to Teresa Noakes. Extracts from Crown Copyright records in the Public Record Office appear by permission of HM Stationery Office.

1 The Background

A second Elizabethan age: illusion and reality

The timing of the demise of King George VI on 6 February 1952 was something of a misfortune for his country. For it brought to the throne a young monarch who stood in considerable apparent contrast to her father and as a result caused many of her subjects to suppose that her accession might somehow mark a turning point in the country's fortunes and inaugurate a national revival. We now know that this was a collective self-delusion which, if anything, added to the country's problems.

The reign of George VI had begun inauspiciously in 1936 in the wake of the abdication of King Edward VIII and had been marked by many tribulations. Soon followed the disagreeable process of 'throwing Czechoslovakia to the German wolves', something with which the new King and Queen saw fit publicly to identify themselves by parading on the balcony of Buckingham Palace with their Prime Minister, Neville Chamberlain, to acknowledge the cheers of the crowds on the occasion of his return from Munich. Next came the Second World War and its troubled aftermath. True, Great Britain achieved victory of a kind in the wars with Germany, Italy and Japan, and there was even heady talk of the country having experienced its finest hour. But the reality was that the exertions involved had fatally undermined national finances and made inevitable the abandonment in the immediate post-war years of the Indian Sub-Continent, which had traditionally been seen as the brightest jewel in the imperial crown. Also unavoidable was the need to seek support from the United States, the only unambiguous victor in the Second World War. This was symbolized in dollar loans, in the handing over to the Americans of responsibility for the defence of Greece and Turkey against Communist insurgency (the Truman Doctrine) and in the reluctant decision to terminate the British Mandate in Palestine under pressure from Washington.

For most of George VI's subjects, however, the principal feature of his reign was the almost unrelenting austerity that prevailed from the outbreak of war to the time of his death. As late as October 1951, for example, the weekly food ration per person[1] was:

Bacon and ham	3 oz
Cheese	$1\frac{1}{2}$ oz
Butter	3 oz
Margarine	4 oz
Cooking fat	2 oz
Meat	1s 7d worth
Sugar	10 oz
Tea	2 oz
Chocolates and sweets	$6\frac{1}{2}$ oz

George VI's Great Britain, then, had turned into a grey, shabby and almost beleaguered island with many of its people already well prepared to face a future of inevitable decline in the face of legions of reviving competitors.

Seen in this context, the timing of the accession of Queen Elizabeth II can only be retrospectively regretted. For too many of her subjects came to discern the false dawn of a possible British renaissance. Such was the contrast between the bright, articulate, youthful daughter and the sombre, inadequate, stuttering father that talk of a Second Elizabethan Age became an inevitable media obsession during the 16 months between her accession and her Coronation. And the Coronation itself, attended by a glittering array of personalities drawn from the many remaining British Dominions and Colonies, gave a superficial impression of continuity with the great Victorian past. But it was to be no more than the beginning of an 'Indian Summer'. For Great Britain's 'Antonine Age' had gone for ever. This was not to be sufficiently recognized, however, until 1956 when the humiliation that was the Suez Affair cruelly punctured most of the country's remaining pretensions to being a power of the first rank. By the mid-1980s Britain had been 'diminished to fourteenth place in the non-communist world in terms of Gross National Product per head ... with little more than a third of West Germany's manu-facturing output per head and a half that of the United States; with mass unemployment standing at over 13 per cent of the insured population, a rate one-third worse than in West Germany and four times worse than in Japan'.[2]

More illusions were no doubt also fostered both at home and abroad by the symbolic presence at the Coronation of the young sovereign's first Prime Minister, Winston Churchill, then nearing 80. Having entered Parliament in 1900 and having served in the Cabinet before the First World War, he was the living embodiment of national aspirations to believe that the two world wars had been triumphantly successful crusades for high principle. Many even dared to hope that under his renewed leadership Great Britain might be put on track to leave behind the age of austerity and to re-establish itself as the world power of former times. Among the optimists was Churchill himself.

During his second tenure at 10 Downing Street (from October 1951 to April 1955) various developments could have been interpreted as providing tentative confirmation that a major British renaissance was indeed in progress. At home, for example, advantage was taken of the ending of the Korean War and a favourable turn in the balance of trade to increase general living standards and to end rationing. Moreover, full employ-ment and a fair degree of industrial peace appeared to have become established features of the political landscape.[3] And in the global arena the country's decline, so apparent during the years of Clement Attlee's Labour government (1945–51), might have been seen as having been arrested. There was now no need to seek dollar loans, and enforced devaluation was not apparently threatened. Colonial unrest also seemed capable of being contained. And as for the Cold War, Joseph Stalin's death in 1953 seemed to have ushered in a period of relative tranquillity symbolized by the termination on honourable terms for the West of the Korean War. This in turn led Churchill to argue that a three-power Summit, modelled on those held during the Second World War at Teheran, Yalta and Potsdam, had become desirable. That he himself intended to play a *beau rôle* at such a Summit went of course without saying. In the event, because of lack of American enthusiasm, the Summit was not to materialize until after Churchill's retirement. But in the feverish discussion of the subject during 1953 and 1954 there was never any question that the British, under Churchill's leadership, were entitled to an equal place of honour at the world's top table. In short, the bilateral super-power Summits, with which we are now so familiar, would have been unthinkable in the early 1950s. Indeed, the very term 'superpower', used to describe the United States and the Soviet Union, had not yet come into vogue. The British could thus cling to their illusions for a few years longer. But 'no end of a lesson' awaited them in 1956.

The underlying reality in Churchill's 'Indian Summer' was, we can now see, decidedly sombre. The Prime Minister, with his immense global prestige, could not of course be expected to go on for ever. And once he had gone it was unlikely, with or without the Suez disaster, that the Americans and the Soviets would for long have been prepared to acknowledge as anything like an equal a country which no longer had any comparable power base. True, Great Britain was a front-rank global power if judged by its commitments. But it was certainly not so if judged by its capacity to fulfil them. In short, the modest economic recovery of the early 1950s could not possibly erase the memory of the sheer financial necessity that had led the British to quit India and Palestine and had caused them to foist the main burden of waging the Cold War, whether in Europe or in Asia, onto the Americans.

At the heart of the matter lay the question of the nature of the 'special relationship' with the United States. Churchill wanted a partnership of equals or near-equals. In 1946, in his famous speech at Fulton, Missouri, he had set out his views with engaging candour:

Let no man underrate the abiding power of the British Empire and Commonwealth ... do not suppose that we shall not come through these dark years of privation as we have come through the glorious years of agony or that half a century from now [1996!] you will not see 70,000,000 or 80,000,000 of Britons spread around the world and united in defence of our tradition, our way of life and of the world cause we and you [the Americans] espouse. ...

If the population of the English-speaking Commonwealth be added to that of the United States, with all that such co-operation implies in the air, on the sea and in science and industry, there will be no quivering, precarious balance of power to offer temptation to ambition or adventure. On the contrary, there will be an overwhelming assurance of security.

If we adhere faithfully to the Charter of the United Nations and walk forward in sedate strength, seeking no one's land or treasure or seeking to lay no arbitrary control on the thoughts of men, if all British moral and material forces and convictions are joined with your own in fraternal association, the high roads of the future will be clear, not only for us but for all, not only for our time but for a century to come.[4]

Back in office after 1951 he showed little sign of having modified his views of what was likely to be acceptable to the Americans. Hence he rejected the idea of Great Britain joining any European Federation and insisted, in common with most of his compatriots in all political parties, that the country's destiny was to serve as a mediating force between the North American and West European pillars of the North Atlantic Alliance. The fact that no leading American wanted a 'special relationship' on these terms was simply not to be countenanced. It must, then, be supposed that Churchill would have been devastated if he could have read what Dwight D. Eisenhower wrote in his diary on the eve of becoming American President in 1953:

Mr Churchill is as charming and interesting as ever, but he is quite definitely showing the effects of the passing years. He has fixed in his mind a certain international relationship he is trying to establish – possibly it would be better to say an atmosphere he is trying to create. This is that Britain and the British Commonwealth are not to be treated just as other nations would be treated by the United States in our complicated foreign problems. On the contrary, he most earnestly hopes and intends that those countries shall enjoy a relationship which will recognize the special place of partnership they occupied with us during World War II. . . .

In those days he had the enjoyable feeling that he and our President were sitting on some rather Olympian platform with respect to the rest of the world, and directing world affairs from that point of vantage. Even if this picture were an accurate one of those days, it would have no application to the present. . . .

In the present international complexities, any hope of establishing such a relationship is completely fatuous.[5]

In Churchill's time, however, no leading American, not even Eisenhower, was ever willing to tell the British in so many words that their vision of the 'special relationship' was 'completely fatuous'. Only later, under another Prime Minister, would the Americans spell out in unmistakable fashion that any 'special relationship' would have to be based on the British being little more than auxiliaries or subalterns rather than equals or near-equals. In this, as in so much else, Churchill was to bequeath a *damnosa hereditas*. And Anthony Eden was destined to be the hapless heir.

The early 1950s also saw a transition taking place in the Mother Country's relations with the Dominions. But once again the full extent of what was happening was only to be made evident *after* Churchill's retirement. Ever since 1931, with the passing of the Statute of Westminster, the Old Dominions of Canada, Australia, New Zealand and South Africa had in theory possessed full sovereign rights to shape their own international policies. But in 1939 there was no serious doubt, except possibly in the case of South Africa, that all would show solidarity with the Mother Country when war with Germany was imminent. In the post-war era, however, Great Britain's diminishing world role did not pass unnoticed. Canada had already by 1945 come to accept that in security matters its future was inextricably linked not with London but with Washington. And Australia and New Zealand had tacitly begun to travel the same road when in 1951 they forged with the Americans the so-called ANZUS Pact, from which the British were pointedly excluded. As for South Africa, the decisive electoral victory of the Dutch-descended element in

1948 put it on a path that made any loyalty to London increasingly nominal.

The members of the New Commonwealth – India, Pakistan and Ceylon – were also by no means inclined to play the role of dutiful daughters. But the full extent of their willingness to defy London had still not been revealed when Churchill retired in 1955. A clear indication of what might be in store, however, came later in that same year when Jawaharlal Nehru, the Indian Prime Minister, saw fit to play a prominent role in the Bandung Conference of non-aligned nations. Together with Gamal Abdel Nasser of Egypt and Josip Broz Tito of Yugoslavia, he propagated the virtues of positive neutralism in world affairs, pointedly ignoring Great Britain's role in NATO. The portents for Great Britain's ability to lead its Commonwealth without challenge were thus far from auspicious in the early 1950s. But once again a showdown was not to occur until the Suez Crisis of 1956.

As well as presiding uneasily over a Commonwealth of independent states, Great Britain also still had control over a vast collection of dependent colonies in the 1950s. No clear policy had yet been enunciated about their long-term future when Churchill retired. That some would follow India down the path to complete independence was acknowledged. But there was much uncertainty about timing. And in the case of at least one colony – Cyprus – a government minister felt that 'never' was the appropriate term to employ. Resistance to colonial rule in certain cases was, of course, expected but there was no consensus in London that invariably repression was ultimately bound to prove a hopeless response. For some the lesson of the Malayan Emergency was that a firm and skilful campaign by the colonial power might succeed in routing troublemakers. But in any case few serious challenges to British authority were in progress during Churchill's 'Indian Summer', the Mau Mau Campaign in Kenya being a striking exception and one, incidentally, which the British authorities had high hopes of containing.

Great Britain's 'informal empire' in the Middle East

It is right to state, however, that the ultimate fate of most of the colonies still remaining under formal British rule in the early 1950s seems in retrospect to have been of only marginal importance to the well-being or otherwise of the majority of the inhabitants of the Mother Country. Once the Indian Sub-Continent had been lost, most of what remained of the formal Empire was of central importance neither from a strategic nor an economic perspective. What *was* perceived to be of vital concern was the perpetuation of British influence in a region where scarcely any full-blown colonies had ever existed, namely the Middle East. The overriding need was held to be ensuring the flow of oil from there not only to Great Britain but to other West European states as well. For this was an era when the North Sea oilfields had not been developed and when the precarious post-war economic recovery of Great Britain and her non-Communist neighbours was thought to be wholly dependent on the availability of Middle East oil at the pre-vailing give-away prices.

At the end of the Second World War the British policy-making elite, with the almost unquestioning support of Attlee's Labour government, had taken for granted that the British would be able to continue the necessary predominance over the Middle East which had been essential to victory in two world wars and which had, if anything, apparently been strengthened by the catastrophies endured during the Second World War by erstwhile regional rivals, France and Germany. Hence, just as the British were reconciling themselves to the need to surrender the brightest jewel in their formal Empire, namely the Indian Sub-Continent, they were simultaneously preparing to strengthen their grip on the brightest jewel in their 'informal empire', namely the system of client relationships they had developed with such varied Middle Eastern states as Egypt, Iran, Jordan and Iraq.

Yet in the first post-war decade the realization dawned on the British that they faced a variety of challenges in the Middle East that were in practice to be as daunting as anything experienced during the last years of the Indian Raj. For some in London the most serious threat appeared to come, ironically, from the United States which in the European theatre was becoming such a steadfast ally. That the 'special relationship' did not seem to be working in the Middle East in the same happy fashion was attributed by some not so much to politicians in Washington as to commercial forces on Wall Street who saw opportunities to muscle in on a British sphere of influence. Saudi Arabia, in particular, was seen as being encouraged by irresponsible Americans to intrigue against British client regimes. But even the American political leaders were much criticized in London for failing to condemn sufficiently the anti-British conduct of the Iranians in 1951. Led by Mohammed Mussadiq, the latter simply nationalized the oil wells which had been developed by the British-owned Anglo-Iranian Oil Company (AIOC) and defied the British to send the traditional gunboats. Lacking American support, the Attlee government backed away from a confrontation but were much criticized at home for alleged weakness. The Prime Minister himself made clear to his Cabinet on 27 September 1951 that he did not think it expedient to use force 'in view of the attitude of the United States Government'.[6] Once Churchill had returned to the premiership, however, Anglo-American policies were for a time rather fortuitously brought into harmony and a successful joint conspiracy was mounted in 1953 to remove Mussadiq from power. But there was a price to pay which many in London resented: the Americans had to be given an equal share in exploiting Iranian oil which had hitherto been the sole preserve of the AIOC.

For many British experts, however, a greater threat to their Middle Eastern interests was seen as ultimately coming not so much from the Americans as from the Soviets. While initially almost completely without influence or presence in the region, Moscow was held by many to be only waiting for an opportunity to pounce. The response to this was held in London to lie in the development of the collective defence potential of the region under British leadership. Some countries in the Middle East eventually showed a willingness to accept this thesis and offered full cooperation with the British. They were to be led by

Turkey and Iraq. But one country, in particular, was to show steady resistance to British plans for developing a NATO of the Middle East. This was Egypt which, as bad luck would have it, was then the most influential Moslem country in the region. And without Egyptian support for a collective defence arrangement, many smaller countries, including even Jordan, were inclined to waver.

Why did Egypt set out to foil British plans? A part of the explanation – much favoured among the 'Arabists' in the British Foreign Office – derived from the creation of Israel in 1948. The British had consistently resisted mass Jewish immigration into Palestine before, during and after the Second World War. And they had in practice opposed the idea of creating a Jewish state there, whatever Arthur Balfour may have said in 1917. But in 1948 they felt compelled to agree to surrender the League of Nations Mandate over Palestine awarded to them at the end of the First World War and to acquiesce in the partition solution favoured by an American-led majority in the United Nations. Financial difficulty was one factor explaining this capitulation by Great Britain in an area where it was supposedly the dominant Great Power. And another was pressure from the Zionist-influenced Administration of Harry S. Truman in Washington, whose support in Western Europe was desperately required. The Egyptians, in particular, resented this alleged British betrayal of the Arab cause. And they even sought by armed force to prevent Israel coming into existence. This turned out to be a fatal error as the attempt failed and, moreover, led to the loss to Israel of further territory originally designated as Arab. A fundamental tenet of Egyptian foreign policy for the next quarter of a century was thus created: anti-Zionism would predominate over anti-Communism. The British, as friends of the Americans, were suspected, usually unjustly, of sympathizing with Israel. In such circumstances, according to many British 'Arabists', no British-dominated collective defence organization was likely to have any lasting appeal in Cairo. This led some in the British policy-making elite to favour a line of trying to appease the Egyptians by working for an Arab–Israeli settlement which, while not actually destroying the Jewish state, would reduce its size and meet at least some Arab desiderata. As will be seen, British supporters of this approach began to hope for serious progress in 1955 when the Americans, now led by a less Zionist-influenced President than Truman, also surprisingly came to favour putting pressure on Israel to compromise with its enemies. Initiatives in this direction soon foundered, however, as tensions leading to the Suez Crisis of 1956 intensified. But it seems doubtful in any case whether an Israeli–Egyptian peace settlement, even if achieved, would really have made much difference to the Anglo-Egyptian relationship and thus have opened the way for Egyptian participation in an anti-Soviet collective defence arrangement.

What the optimists in the 'Arabist-minded' British Foreign Office seem to have been unwilling to contemplate was the possibility that by the 1950s the majority of Egyptians of whatever class were simply viscerally anti-British whatever happened about Israel and that they had no sincere desire for any kind of long-term security arrangements with London whether against the Soviet Union or any other power. This seems to have applied no less to the monarchical regime of King Farouk than to the regime of middle-class officers which took over in 1952. The British Foreign Office could not accept this. Some American observers, especially those in contact with the American Embassy in Cairo, do seem, however, to have grasped that this was probably the unvarnished truth. For example, Burton Y. Berry, Deputy Assistant Secretary in the US State Department, wrote after a visit to Egypt: 'I found a terrible situation. The British are detested. The hatred against them is general and intense. It is shared by everyone in the country.'[7]

Why, then, might the British by the early 1950s have been so hated by the Egyptians (and to a lesser extent throughout the Middle East)? The root cause was that the British had conquered Egypt in 1882 and had remained in at least partial occupation of the country ever since. True, the original conquest was undertaken by the Liberal government of W. E. Gladstone with the utmost reluctance following rioting in which numerous Egyptians had been killed and the ruling Khedive Ismail was held to stand in need of support against allegedly extremist domestic forces. It was intended to be of a purely temporary character, and numerous attempts had been made between 1882 and 1954 to negotiate an end to the occupation of some or all of Egypt's territory. In 1922, for example, the British piously declared that they recognized Egypt as an independent state. And in 1936 the young Eden, then Stanley Baldwin's Foreign Secretary, successfully negotiated an Anglo-Egyptian Treaty which aspired to a total British withdrawal of troops within 20 years 'provided they were no longer needed' and which also provided for formal 'renewal or review' by 1956. And following some rather traumatic events in wartime Cairo, the British eventually showed themselves to be as good as their word by actually quitting Cairo and Alexandria in 1947 and by offering to leave even the sensitive Suez Canal Zone by 1949, something the Egyptians astonishingly turned down when the British did not also consent to hand over the Sudan at the same time. Thus, seen through many eyes in London, continuous British presence in Egypt since 1882 had been fortuitous rather than the result of a calculated imperialist design to conquer and subjugate. Most Egyptians, however, were unwilling to see matters in this light: the British record was held to be one of unrelenting hypocrisy and hence no genuine friend-ship or long-term security cooperation was even to be contemplated.

For the British, the prospects of an agreement of some kind seemed suddenly to improve in July 1952. For a coup led by army officers forced King Farouk to abdicate. And the new government, headed by General Mohammed Neguib and Colonel Nasser (the latter soon superseding the former as virtual dictator), proved willing to abandon King Farouk's long-standing claim to Egyptian sovereignty over the Sudan. This overcame the impasse which had prevented the Attlee government from withdrawing all forces from Egypt. By now, however, Churchill was back as Prime Minister and he dis-approved of the policy he had inherited. All the same, he reluctantly consented to recommend a treaty involving troop withdrawal when faced with the insistence of his Cabinet colleagues, led by Foreign Secretary Eden, that failure to agree to leave the Canal Zone would provoke major guerrilla warfare with cost implications that could not be countenanced. Thus it was that in July 1954 Heads of Agreement were signed requiring all British forces to leave Egypt by 18 June 1956. Provision was made that such forces could return to the Canal Zone only if an Arab state or Turkey should be attacked by an outside power (excluding Israel).

Eden, as the principal architect of the agreement, hoped that a new era in Anglo-Egyptian relations might soon open. In particular, he could see no good reason why Egypt should not eventually come to appreciate that its interests lay in tacit cooperation with or even participation in a British-led regional security pact. But this was to misread the lesson of earlier attempts to involve the Egyptians in something of this kind in the course of the negotiations for British troop withdrawal. All British efforts, backed initially by the Americans, to interest the Neguib regime in joining a Middle East Defence Organization (MEDO) had fallen on deaf ears. And this Egyptian outlook was not to change after 1954. For the new regime in Cairo had determined to espouse a form of Arabic nationalism whose prospects depended on mobilizing anti-British feeling throughout the Middle East. Thus the fall of King Farouk, though the key to ending the Sudanese impasse, opened the way to a far more menacing regional challenge to London at a time when Eden was about to succeed Churchill as Prime Minister.

Eden's personal identification, in the face of Churchill's known scepticism, with the 1954 Treaty was of seminal importance. For it meant that the new Prime Minister would feel an acute sense of personal betrayal when the Egyptian challenge to the entire British position in the Middle East materialized. Moreover, he could not easily forget that in 1954 his course had been bitterly opposed by a sizeable group of Conservative backbenchers who were likely to be a thorn in his flesh if he continued to prefer 'appeasement' to 'confrontation'. This was the so-called 'Suez Group' led by Captain Charles Waterhouse and Julian Amery.

'Appeasement' was a charge that Eden found difficult to face. For he himself had resigned from the Cabinet in February

1938 in protest at Neville Chamberlain's alleged 'appease-ment' of Fascist Italy. Churchill in his war memoirs had written of this resignation:

> my heart sank and for a while the dark waters of despair overwhelmed me ... During all the war soon to come and in all its darkest times I never had any trouble sleeping ... But now on this night ... and on this occasion only sleep deserted me. From midnight till dawn I lay in my bed consumed by emotions of sorrow and fear. There seemed one strong young figure standing up against long, dismal, drawling tides of drift and surrender.[8]

With endorsement of this kind Eden had easily emerged as Churchill's heir apparent. But there was an obvious price to pay: his own performance in the highest office would be judged by unusually, perhaps impossibly, high standards. The last thing he needed, once his gamble with the Egyptians was seen to have failed, was a group of Conservative critics comparing him with Chamberlain rather than Churchill.

If only British political opinion had been as unified and consistently hostile to Egypt as it had been to Nazi Germany and Fascist Italy during the Second World War, Eden's problem would have been relatively easy: he could simply have declared that Nasser was revealing himself to be a new Adolf Hitler or Benito Mussolini and set out to resist him. But no such consistent hostility was present in the Great Britain of the 1950s. The fact was that the nation had for some years been fatally polarized on the central issues involved. The attitudes espoused by the Conservative 'Suez Group' had a fair follow-ing, not least among those of all classes and all voting habits who had served in North Africa during the Second World War. There was also, however, significant support for both 'anti-imperialist Little Englandism' and for 'high-minded inter-nationalism'. And such support was particularly widespread among intellectuals and among political activists in the Labour and Liberal Parties.

The roots of such thinking are not easily traced. But the anti-imperialist tradition appears to go back at least as far as the 'Little Englanders' of the mid-nineteenth century. This had been greatly strengthened after the Second World War when the leaders of the Labour government had made a virtue of necessity in withdrawing from the Indian Sub-Continent. It became eminently fashionable to fulminate against those less 'enlightened' politicians who appeared to believe in 'gunboat diplomacy'. Churchill and others could counter with charges of 'scuttle' but the *Zeitgeist* appeared to be against them. At all events, in 1951 the *Daily Mirror* thought it would sway votes away from the Conservatives by asking 'Whose Finger on the Trigger?' in the context of the Iranian oil crisis.

A second important strand of thinking with which any exponent of 'gunboat diplomacy' had to contend in the 1950s was that which held that the rule of law should always prevail in international affairs and that Great Britain, in particular, had a duty to show a noble example. These ideas can be traced back at least to Gladstone's philippics against Benjamin Disraeli in the 1870s. And they certainly inspired an important inter-war pressure group, the League of Nations Union, which clamoured for a high-minded British lead against various acts of aggression and, in particular, against the Italian attack on Abyssinia in defiance of the League of Nations. True, some of those concerned, influenced by pacifist or quasi-pacifist sentiments, were doubtful whether military force should ever be used. But in the end most British supporters of this kind of internationalism lined up with the Conservative anti-appeasers and welcomed the British declaration of war on behalf of Poland in 1939. Most leading Conservative anti-appeasers, including probably both Churchill and Eden, were less than convinced believers in noble internationalism. But satisfied that the national interest required resistance to the Fascist dictators, they found it prudent to mouth such slogans as 'Arms and the [League] Covenant' in the eventually successful attempt to win allies on the Left who would help them to oust Chamberlain, whose interpretation of the national interest differed from theirs. Eden, in particular, had at this period built a reputation as a supporter of the League of Nations and the rule of law in international relations. And in the post-war years he also paid appropriate lip service to the United Nations, even at one point being considered for the post of Secretary-General.

Thus when Eden became Prime Minister in April 1955 he was not well placed at home to face the challenge represented by Nasser. For there was really no reconciling the forces of the Conservative 'Suez Group' with those of the high-minded internationalists who had a fair following in all three political parties. Yet both groups looked to Eden to be true to a tradition to which they thought he ought to belong: in the one case that of espousing the stout defence of national interest as understood by Conservatives since the time of Disraeli; in the other case that of suspicion of old-fashioned imperialism and loyalty to the rule of law in international affairs.

But what of Eden's capacity to face this uniquely difficult situation? This question presents a singular challenge to historians and political scientists seeking to generalize about leadership in pluralistic democracies. For Eden's personal history and characteristics, on a superficial reading, may seem to invite every kind of sweeping judgement. And the course of the Suez Affair was so dramatic and its outcome so self-evidently catastrophic as to have appeared to some commentators to justify the most lurid kind of explanations, namely that British leadership had fallen into the hands of someone who, for whatever reason, had virtually lost his sanity.

Anthony Eden: a vulnerable Prime Minister?

Those seeking to explain the Suez Affair largely in terms of Eden's personal history may wish to stress that his earlier life was packed with personal tragedies. True, he reached his eighteenth year before the loss of one of his parents (his father), an unusual occurrence among modern British Prime Ministers as Lucille Iremonger has pointed out.[9] But that his childhood was nevertheless unusually troubled is undoubted. As early as 1933 his brother, Sir Timothy Eden, published an account of the irrational rages of their father, Sir William Eden. He recalled that 'he took a marked delight in embarrassing those with whom he talked, and he spared no one, neither for their helplessness nor their strength, man, woman or child, peer or peasant, from his sweeping condemnation or his biting ridicule'. He recorded without disbelief that his father had been accused of having bitten a carpet. And he revealed something of the strain faced by Sir William's children when he wrote: 'Nor will anyone readily admit that the whistling of a boy in the street can be a good or sufficient reason for breaking a window with a flower-pot.'[10] As for his unloving mother, we learn from Eden's 'authorized' biographer, Robert Rhodes James, that she also caused constant distress to her offspring by her financial irresponsibility and consequent degrading involvement with money-lenders.[11] And Eden himself wrote of her: 'I think my mother preferred the simpler relationship which existed between donor and recipient to the more complicated one between mother and child.'[12] Eden also had to live with doubts, still unsettled, as to his parentage: rumour had it that his real father was not Sir William Eden but George Wyndham.

The First World War also brought its share of suffering to Eden and may have contributed to making him the highly strung Prime Minister he undoubtedly was. Two of his three brothers were killed in action and he himself often came close to death on the Western Front. He wrote to his surviving brother from the trenches following the death of his father and his other two brothers:

Should I be killed before I see you again, remember this always – I shall be with Jack, Nicholas and Daddie, and although I may be for a time here in this earth I shall be with others. I shall be *so* happy with them, I *know* I shall.

I can barely write tonight, I am in such a curious mood.

I feel almost hysterical, it all seems so cruel, and yet I know they are all much happier in paradise.

But my heart aches at times at the horror of it all.[13]

Back in peacetime Great Britain, Eden entered Parliament in 1923 and in the same year married Beatrice Beckett. The marriage brought him much distress. 'I do not know', writes Rhodes James, 'when it was that Eden discovered Beatrice was having affairs with other men, but it was depressingly early in their marriage.'[14] Separation and eventual divorce became inevitable – then no easy thing for an ambitious politician to face.

Another great trauma came in 1945 when his elder son, Simon, went missing in action in Burma. During the Potsdam Conference Eden was required to carry out his duties as Foreign Secretary with the fate of his son in the balance. Then on 20 July he received confirmation that the worst had happened. Lord Moran, Churchill's doctor, wrote that he was warned by the Prime Minister in advance of a dinner that Eden had just heard the news: 'They talked until midnight as if nothing had happened. I wonder if I could have behaved with the same quiet dignity . . . ?'[15]

The post-war years brought more troubles for Eden. Kept out of the leadership of the Conservative Party (and later out of the premiership) between 1945 and 1955 by a selfish and arguably senile Churchill, he became increasingly desperate not to miss the supreme prize. His partnership with Churchill accordingly deteriorated and bore no resemblance to the father-and-son relationship of popular myth. Then in 1953 Eden's health broke down. He had never enjoyed really excellent health and had occasionally had to take periods of enforced rest, for example in April 1944 and in June 1945 (on the latter occasion with a duodenal ulcer). During the Second World War, in particular, he had driven himself too hard. The diary of his Private Secretary, Oliver Harvey, reveals beyond doubt that he should not have attempted to be both Foreign Secretary and Leader of the House at the same time.[16] In addition, he was plagued by having to spend endless post-prandial sessions with Churchill. These often lasted until the early hours and were usually more concerned with the Prime Minister's personal reminiscences than with vital decisions relating to the war. Churchill himself compensated for these late hours by regularly taking an afternoon nap, something Eden felt he had to deny himself. Health may also have been a factor in causing Eden to resign as Neville Chamberlain's Foreign Secretary in February 1938, though he himself always denied it. Malcolm MacDonald has written in the following terms about his efforts to dissuade Eden from resigning:

Late in the afternoon of the day when Cabinet meetings had failed to reconcile the difference of view between Chamberlain and Eden and when the efforts of a group of other ministers to persuade Eden to change his mind about resigning from the government had also failed, Chamberlain suggested to me that I should have a talk with Eden in a final attempt to dissuade him from his proposed course. I agreed to do this. Eden and I were cordial personal friends and ministerial colleagues who had often co-operated together in the context of the government's international policies. . . .

Eden gladly came to dinner with me. Through the meal and for a long time afterwards as we sipped drinks we discussed the current problem. I expressed the reasons why I thought that he should not resign on the issue which had arisen. He restated the reasons why he thought he should do so; and we exchanged arguments and counter-arguments in a very friendly way. Sometimes he agreed with a point which I made, but then shifted his comments to another aspect of the subject. Usually he stayed firm in his opinion, but just now and then he appeared perhaps to be prepared to reconsider his decision, and to continue serving as the Foreign Secretary. Then, at one of those moments he suddenly shook his head rather desperately and said that although there was much to be said for my point of view he could not continue working as a Minister because he did not feel fit to do so; he felt physically unwell and mentally exhausted. (I do not now remember the exact words that he used, but that was the substance of his remark.)

He might have been making an excuse for not being persuaded by me to alter his decision; but by then I did not think this was the reason for his sudden somewhat emotional outburst. During our talk I felt increasingly worried about the state of his mind. His thoughts seemed to be less clear and reasonably coherent than they usually were, and his statements were occasionally somewhat confused. I began to wonder whether he was well enough to continue performing the difficult tasks of his supremely important office through the critical times which lay ahead. When he made that remark I decided that it would in fact be better if he did resign.

Before the Cabinet met the next morning I went to see the Prime Minister in 10 Downing Street. I told him that my efforts to persuade Eden to change his mind had failed – and that indeed by the end of my talk with him it was I who had changed my mind. I said that I thought that he was too mentally and physically exhausted to continue working wisely and well in his high office, and that in the circumstances, however regrettable, it would be better if he did resign.

Chamberlain smiled and said he had 'slept on the matter', and had come to the same conclusion.[17]

Is there perhaps here some evidence to bolster claims about alleged mental instability on the part of the 'architect of Suez'?

In 1953, however, Eden's breakdown was much more dramatic than anything that had gone before, but it was essentially physical not mental in character if such a distinction is in order. Certainly, its severity was of a purely physical nature and depended on pure chance. For, as a result of a surgeon's error in a gallbladder operation, his bile duct was cut. This necessitated further operations, including one in the United States, before he could return, after six month's absence, to the Foreign Office. For the rest of his life he was to be subject to occasional fevers necessitating the use of drugs. One such fever occurred during the course of the Suez Crisis and has led to what are, it seems, largely false or at least unprovable assumptions that his broad conduct of high policy at that period was crucially affected.

Two other matters must be mentioned. According to Kennett Love, Clarissa, Eden's second wife, had a miscarriage in the course of the Suez Crisis.[18] This is neither confirmed nor denied by his 'authorized' biographer, who mentions, however, a miscarriage in 1954 ('a keenly felt tragedy').[19] If she did indeed have a miscarriage in 1956 the question may be asked whether the stress involved combined with Eden's bile duct problem to affect his judgement. Finally, the point is often made that Eden regularly lost sleep during the Suez Crisis because of the need to take telephone calls from Washington and New York (the United Nations) which are, of course, five hours behind London. Could simple exhaustion explain his many alleged misjudgements?

How relevant is all this to the course of the Suez Crisis? It seems impossible to identify any particular decision that could be ascribed to anything other than intellectual conviction on Eden's part that it was correct in the circumstances. In short, it cannot be demonstrated that his fevers, his wife's supposed miscarriage, his unhappy childhood, his divorce or the like made any discernible difference. The most that can safely be said is that these factors may have contributed, *with many other factors* (*knowable and unknowable*), to make Eden the person he was during 1956. But they explain nothing in particular in the history of the Suez Crisis.

Two further observations. First, too much can be made of Eden's notorious irascibility and temperament. That he was inconsiderate to subordinates is undoubted, as the diary of Sir Evelyn Shuckburgh illustrates.[20] But he never went to such extremes as to lead to general doubts about his sanity. (No proof has emerged supporting claims that he threw inkpots at people.) In any case, the Suez Crisis matured over many months, so that its course is hardly attributable to any momentary loss of temper on Eden's part. Likewise, claims that he was unusually highly strung and disposed to engage in constant, even neurotic, interference in the work of his colleagues really do not explain anything in particular about a major national issue like Suez.

A final question: did Eden in confronting Nasser see himself as some kind of hero in politics resulting in the absence of normal perspective on his part? After all, he had won a Military Cross in the First World War. And in politics he was widely acclaimed (once appeasement was held to have failed) for resigning from Chamberlain's pre-war Cabinet; and he appeared to have the blessing, when becoming Prime Minister in 1955, of the supposedly toweringly heroic Churchill. Yet the fact was that he had *not* risen to the top by engaging in incautious heroics. For him, as for most successful British politicians who have seen action in war, politics was *not* a replay of the Somme. He had been a protégé of Baldwin not Churchill or Lloyd George. He had been Foreign Secretary while Mussolini was conquering Abyssinia and while Hitler was remilitarizing the Rhineland. His resignation from Chamberlain's Cabinet had been over a relatively obscure issue. He had been less than heroic in the period from his resignation until the outbreak of war. And even with respect to Nasser, whom he eventually came to hate, he had originally, as we have seen, been extremely accommodating.

The conclusion seems inevitable: Eden was a more normal and a more cautious British peacetime politician than is usually acknowledged. It was the character of the Suez Crisis itself that was exceptional.

Notes

1 Conservative and Unionist Central Office, *The Campaign Guide, 1955* (London, 1955), p. 179.
2 Correlli Barnett, *The Audit of War* (London, 1986), pp. 7–8.
3 For details see Anthony Seldon, *Churchill's Indian Summer: the Conservative Government, 1951—55* (London, 1981).
4 *The Times*, 6 March 1946.
5 Eisenhower Diary, 5 January 1953, Eisenhower Library, Abilene, Kansas, quoted in David Carlton, *Anthony Eden: a Biography* (London, 1981), pp. 332–3.
6 Cab. 128/20, Public Record Office (PRO). For further details see William Roger Louis, *The British Empire in the Middle East, 1945—1951: Arab Nationalism, the United States and Postwar Imperialism* (London, 1984).
7 Quoted in Louis, *The British Empire in the Middle East*, p. 742.
8 Winston S. Churchill, *The Second World War* (6 vols, London, 1948–54), vol. 1, p. 221.
9 Lucille Iremonger, *The Fiery Chariot: a Study of British Prime Ministers and the Search for Love* (London, 1970).
10 Timothy Eden, *The Tribulations of a Baronet* (London, 1933), pp. 22–4.
11 Robert Rhodes James, *Anthony Eden* (London, 1986), esp. pp. 94–5.
12 Anthony Eden, Earl of Avon, *Another World 1897—1917* (London, 1976), p. 31.
13 Rhodes James, *Anthony Eden*, p. 41.
14 Ibid., p. 131.
15 Lord Moran, *Winston Churchill: the Struggle for Survival* (London, 1966), p. 277.
16 John Harvey (ed.), *The War Diaries of Oliver Harvey* (London, 1978).
17 Malcolm MacDonald, personal communication, 24 January 1980, quoted in Carlton, *Anthony Eden*, pp. 129–30.
18 Kennett Love, *Suez: the Twice Fought War* (London, 1969), p. 444.
19 Rhodes James, *Anthony Eden*, pp. 414–15.
20 Evelyn Shuckburgh, *Descent to Suez: Diaries 1951—56* (London, 1986).

2 The Middle East in Ferment, 1955–July 1956

Egypt, Iraq and the Baghdad Pact

On 20 February 1955 Eden, who by now knew that he was only weeks away from becoming Prime Minister, visited Cairo *en route* for a tour of Asia. He invited Nasser for dinner and talks at the British Embassy. This was to be their only personal encounter. It was not a success. One of Nasser's biographers, Mohammed Heikal, has claimed that Eden behaved like 'a prince dealing with vagabonds'.[1] This was almost certainly not Eden's intention and it is likely that Heikal drew an exaggerated picture. Unfortunately, however, the Eton-educated Eden often gave even his own compatriots the impression of speaking *de haut en bas*. So it may be that his patrician manner did grate upon the sensitive Egyptian leader. Moreover, it was surely a mistake on Eden's part to have caused the meeting to be held in the British Embassy given its unhappy historical associations. It would have been wiser – and more in keeping with normal practice – to have encouraged Nasser to play host. Nasser for his part also succeeded in annoying Eden: when the two were posing for photographs the former appeared to take mischievous pleasure in holding the latter's hand in an affectionate fashion that can only be described as highly unusual among statesmen meeting for the first time.

With the benefit of hindsight, however, we can now see that none of this would have mattered much if the substance of their discussion had not been marked by an ominous failure to agree on a central issue. The fundamental divergence arose over

Eden's obvious approval of the conservative-minded government of Iraq led by Nuri es-Said, which had just forged with Turkey an agreement, which came to be known as the Baghdad Pact. The British obviously intended to adhere to this Pact – they did so formally in April 1955 – and hoped then to recruit other Middle Eastern states as well as the United States. At his Cairo meeting with Eden, Nasser made it unmistakably clear, however, that Egypt would not praise the Pact let alone join it and that he resented Iraq being built up into such a central regional role.

For Eden, the Baghdad Pact was to become an obsession. He saw it as the key to the security of the entire Middle East and hence as nearly an equivalent in importance to the North Atlantic Treaty of 1949. Yet there was a clumsiness about his methods of constructing the Middle Eastern arrangement that seems surprising in so experienced a diplomat. The negotiations leading up to the signing in Washington of the North Atlantic Treaty by no fewer than 12 nations had been marked by lengthy and careful preparation. In 1955, by contrast, the Baghdad Pact began with only two participants, neither of them being great powers. Then Great Britain joined, having obviously been active behind the scenes with Turkey and Iraq. Now other states were urged to fall into step on a piecemeal basis, accepting existing rules and recognizing Baghdad as the Pact's headquarters. This was, of course, a way of ensuring that the whole process was dominated and controlled by Great Britain. And, indeed, this might have made sense if Eden was in a position to know that eventual success was assured. But this was not to be the case. For only Pakistan and Iran ever subsequently adhered to the Pact.

That Egypt would stand out was something Eden initially felt able to live with, and hence he did not at first see the Cairo meeting as a total failure. But what astonished him in the ensuing months was that Egypt proved capable of mobilizing vocal opposition to the Pact throughout the Middle East and was able to use nationalistic broadcast propaganda with such sophistication that not one Arab state could be persuaded to join Iraq in membership. For Iraq this was a catastrophe. It not only meant the eventual collapse of the security arrangement

Iraq had pioneered, it also had serious domestic implications. The conservative monarchy in Baghdad was gradually to be destabilized and was eventually overthrown in a bloody coup in 1958. The exclusive association with the British-sponsored Pact proved fatal for the regime.

The other leading conservative Arab monarchies, namely Saudi Arabia and Jordan, escaped this fate in all probability because by not joining the Baghdad Pact they were able to avoid incurring the full wrath of the Nasserite nationalists. In the case of Saudi Arabia a crucial role was played by its American ally. In normal circumstances the United States would have been expected to enthuse over an ostensibly anti-Soviet defence arrangement. But in this case Secretary of State John Foster Dulles was strangely diffident. Urged by Eden to bring the United States into membership, he vacillated. Was this due to envy of the British who had apparently seized the leading role? Or was it genuine doubt whether any arrangement in which the British were so prominent could be expected to carry the necessary amount of Arab support? At all events, the United States never did join the Baghdad Pact and neither did it bring pressure to bear on either Saudi Arabia or Egypt to do so.

Anglo-American relations in the Middle East

As will be seen, relations between Britain and the United States deteriorated dramatically during the Suez Crisis of 1956. But it is necessary to appreciate that they were often really at cross-purposes from the very beginning of the Eden premiership. Even as early as the summer of 1955 acute differences were just below the surface, and not merely over the Baghdad Pact. At the end of 1954 Eden and Dulles, meeting in Paris, had decided to try to use their joint good offices to bring about an Arab–Israeli settlement. Sir Evelyn Shuckburgh of the British Foreign Office and Francis Russell of the US State Department were given the delicate and secret task (code-named Alpha) of trying to find common ground. And during the ensuing months they appeared to be making progress – not least with the Egyptians. By August 1955, however, Dulles had concluded that he must make some public reference to the project. For it would inevitably involve some sacrifice of territory by Israel as the price of Arab recognition and no American Administration could run the risk of offending Zionist forces at home in an election year. With Eisenhower facing a re-election contest in November 1956, there was thus an apparently unanswerable case for facing up to any unpleasantness before the campaigning began. But Eden was unhappy at the way the Americans proposed to handle the matter and was only with difficulty persuaded by his Foreign Secretary, Harold Macmillan, not to dissociate Great Britain from Dulles's speech when it was eventually delivered on 26 August. Sir Ivone Kirkpatrick, the Permanent Under-Secretary at the Foreign Office, had commented to Macmillan: 'There is something in Mr Dulles which particularly irritates the Prime Minister. So you will not be surprised to hear that he is more than annoyed at Mr Dulles's latest antics.'[2]

Dulles's speech on the Alpha Project was in the event politely received throughout the Middle East and hopes were thus raised that some kind of peace settlement, guaranteed by the United States and Great Britain, might be in sight. Then, at the end of September, a thunderbolt from Cairo hit the American and British governments: Nasser and the Soviets had struck a deal whereby Czechoslovakia would supply arms to Egypt. The doctrinaire anti-Communists in Washington, led by Dulles, were aghast. And the British were dismayed at the long-term implications for their regional dominance. Eden's initial reaction, particularly significant in the light of what happened in 1956, was to seek an estimate from the British Ambassador in Cairo, Sir Humphrey Trevelyan, 'as to Nasser's present position, the extent of his support, and the chances of any rival'. The discouraging reply was that 'there are no reliable signs of the regime losing its grip of the situation or its opponents gaining ground'.[3] Arranging for Nasser to suffer the same fate as Mussadiq in 1953 was thus clearly a non-starter at this point. So Eden and the entire Cabinet, made aware by the Foreign Office of the vital stakes in terms of the long-term prospects for cheap oil, finally came round to recognizing that they were in effect in competition with the Soviets for Egypt's goodwill and that they had no practical alternative but to swallow their pride over the arms deal and seek to outbid the Soviets. Macmillan told the Cabinet on 20 October that 'we should adopt a policy of moderation in our dealings with Egypt and we should endeavour to persuade the Americans to do the same'. And Eden declared:

In view of Nasser's dependence on the support of the army in Egypt his decision to accept the Soviet offer was understandable if regrettable. The allocation of the Egyptian High Dam project to the Egyptian consortium, if it could be secured, would be of immense importance in restoring the prestige of the West, and particularly of the older European powers in the Arab world generally. In our dealings with Egypt it could be a trump card.[4]

The name of the game for a brief period, then, was to be 'appeasement'. And Nasser's dream of an Aswan High Dam, designed to electrify and irrigate the Nile Valley, was to be the inducement to improved Egyptian behaviour. The British were in no position, however, to put up more than a fraction of the cost even though they feared that otherwise the Soviets might step in with a generous offer. So now the Americans had to be persuaded that Nasser should be rewarded rather than punished for his misdeeds.

On the following day, 21 October 1955, Eden accordingly summoned Winthrop Aldrich, the American Ambassador in London. The latter recalled:

Eden ... asked me to come to see him on a matter of greatest importance and urgency. Eden told me that the emergency had arisen in connection with the Egyptian proposal, namely that the Russians had offered to finance the dam ... Eden feared this would give the Soviets a dangerous foothold in an area vital to the interests of Great Britain. Eden was obviously greatly agitated. I think his physical condition led to his being even more likely than he had been in the past to exaggerate the urgency of any problem with which he was faced. He had a tendency to feel in every case that a crisis had arisen which required immediate action. He asked me to take up at once with Washington the question of whether the United States would underwrite the obligations which Great Britain would assume in making such a guarantee [of financing the dam].[5]

The upshot was that by December the Americans had rather surprisingly agreed to help and, in association with the World Bank, a joint Anglo-American offer in principle had been made to Nasser. Detailed and complicated negotiations commenced which dragged on over many months but which the British initially supposed were bound to be successful.

Eden was also eager to resume work on the Alpha Project in the hope of appeasing the Egyptians. And to this end, at the Guildhall on 9 November 1955, he made a major speech in which he went further than Dulles had done in publicly calling on the Israelis to abandon large tracts of territory in return for secure and guaranteed frontiers. This pleased the Egyptians as much as it enraged the Israelis.

The dismissal of Glubb

The improvement in Anglo-Egyptian relations was not, however, destined to endure. The crucial moment came on 1 March 1956 when King Hussein of Jordan dismissed General Sir John Glubb as head of his army. Glubb Pasha, as he was known, had been in the post since 1939 and symbolized Jordan's dependency relationship with Great Britain. What in retrospect is surprising is not King Hussein's removal of a foreigner from such a post after he had served for 17 years but rather that, in an age of growing Third World self-respect, he had not done so earlier. What caused dismay to Eden, however, was not the dismissal *per se*. What led him to overreact were two particular aspects of the matter. One was the abrupt and undiplomatic manner in which so distinguished a soldier had been treated. Secondly, and more important, was the belief that the hand of Nasser was behind the move. In any literal sense this, it now seems, was untrue. All the same, propaganda beamed out from Radio Cairo and the general intriguing of Nasserite forces throughout the Middle East had undoubtedly created conditions in which King Hussein was under pressure to distance himself from the British. This had first found expression in acute form at the end of 1955 when Field Marshal Sir Gerald Templer, the Chief of the Imperial

General Staff, had visited Amman to discuss the possibility of the Jordanians adhering to the Baghdad Pact. The upshot had been pro-Nasser rioting and a decision by the Jordanian government to indicate that they would prefer to remain aloof. This was maddening enough to Eden. But now came Glubb's abrupt dismissal, which further served to take King Hussein out of the Nasserite firing-line.

Eden's reaction to this latest blow to British prestige was undoubtedly somewhat intemperate. And, indeed, if we are to believe Sir Anthony Nutting, then Minister of State at the Foreign Office and a protégé of the Prime Minister, his rage at Nasser knew no bounds. Nutting recalled in 1984:

Eden's reaction to Glubb's dismissal was violent. He blamed Nasser and he decided that the world just wasn't big enough to hold both of them. One had to go. He declared that night a personal war on Abdel Nasser. I spent most of that night with him, first in the Cabinet room and then, when he retired to bed, I sat with him and we went on arguing until five o'clock in the morning. He simply would not accept that the dismissal of Glubb was not Nasser's doing. He called me nothing but a Foreign Office clerk and said I didn't understand anything about politics and the implications of this dismissal for Britain and her Prime Minister. At one point he said, 'You won't accept any arguments against Nasser, you are in love with Nasser.' He was becoming irrational.

I decided that I must try and get the Prime Minister to think on positive lines. So, with the help of Foreign Office advisers, I drew up a set of proposals, the effect of which was that we would attempt to consolidate our position in those countries where we had still considerable influence, namely Iraq, the Gulf states and Jordan, and that we would try to quarantine the Nasser influence . . . Some days later I was horrified to get a telephone call over an open line to the Savoy Hotel in which Anthony Eden said, 'What is all this poppycock you have sent me about isolating and quarantining Nasser? Can't you understand that I want Nasser murdered.' He actually used that word.[6]

Eden's 'authorized' biographer, Rhodes James, appears to be sceptical about the reliability of Nutting's account of the Glubb Crisis. And it is certainly right to bear in mind that Nutting remained in the political wilderness after he resigned during the Suez Crisis on 5 November 1956 and that he took it upon himself, in most controversial fashion for a former Minister of the Crown, to reveal various sensational secrets concerning Eden's conduct of affairs in his account of the Suez Affair, entitled *No End of a Lesson*, published in 1967. At the same time, Rhodes James does concede that Eden's initial reaction to the Glubb dismissal was 'one of great anger' and that 'calmer views gradually prevailed'.[7]

This judgement is amply confirmed by the various telegrams sent by Eden to Amman. In particular, Eden vainly sought to secure a change of mind on King Hussein's part by sending this message:

In view of the lifelong and faithful service rendered to Jordan and your family by this officer, I feel my duty to tell Your Majesty that the resentment in Britain at this action will be widespread and deep. I cannot foretell its final consequences upon the relations between our two countries. Therefore I would earnestly ask Your Majesty to suspend this order and allow General Glubb and his fellow officers to continue their loyal service.[8]

Hussein simply ignored the veiled threats and in effect snubbed Eden, who now had to consider whether to cut off aid to Jordan. But the Prime Minister was gradually talked round, not least by Glubb who selflessly downplayed the personal slight and argued that Anglo-Jordanian friendship could survive the episode.

Eventually, Eden agreed to take a line in the House of Commons that amounted to minimizing what had happened. His major speech on 7 March 1955 was, however, poorly delivered and ill received by a large group of Conservative MPs going well beyond his unreconstructed critics in the 'Suez Group'. After the blow represented by the Egyptian arms deal with the Soviet bloc, questions began to be asked about Eden's suitability as Churchill's successor and accusations of 'appeasement' were on many lips. Clearly, Eden could only endure a limited number of further such humiliations before his future as Prime Minister would be brought into question. In these circumstances, Eden seems to have concluded that Nasser had become an arch-enemy and that an eventual showdown appeared to be becoming inevitable.

The Aswan High Dam

In a sense, then, Nutting was right to see the Glubb Crisis as a turning point. Yet Eden was a politician of great experience and by no means incapable of showing flexibility or, as critics had it, indecisiveness. So, even if one believes that Eden had engaged in wild talk about having Nasser murdered, it does not follow that any particular course of events in Anglo-Egyptian relations had become entirely inevitable by March 1956. In any case Eden was not in a position simply to dictate policy but had to carry at least senior members of the Cabinet with him. Two colleagues, in particular, were of central importance at this time. One was Macmillan who had reluctantly given up the Foreign Office and become Chancellor of the Exchequer in December 1955. An advocate of a moderate response to the Czechoslovak–Egyptian arms deal, as we have seen, his position soon shifted and he began to let it be known that his patience with Nasser was exhausted. Possibly the failure of the Templer Mission to Jordan was a turning point for him. But there may be a less exalted explanation for his conduct during the whole of 1956: he may have realized that Eden was becoming vulnerable on Middle Eastern issues to charges of weakness and vacillation and hence he may have deliberately positioned himself to the right of Eden in the hope of eventually replacing him as Prime Minister. The second decisive voice on the Middle East at this period belonged to the new Foreign Secretary, Selwyn Lloyd. A protégé of Eden's, he is sometimes depicted as a mere mouthpiece of his chief. But to see him in this light is probably a mistake. For he himself made a tour of the Middle East in March 1956 and appears quite independently of Eden to have reached the conclusion that Nasser was an inveterate enemy of Great Britain and he so reported to the Cabinet on 21 March.[9] He plainly did not consider that Egypt could be won over by the bribe of the Aswan High Dam finance. He saw, moreover, that Great Britain's friends in the Middle East were likely to be alienated if the rewards for bad behaviour were seen to be greater than those for loyalty to London.

It was, indeed, to be Lloyd, at least as much as Eden, who gave the lead during April and May 1956 in trying once more to secure an alignment with Washington on Middle Eastern matters. The results were uneven. On Saudi Arabia differences remained. In particular, the British would not support Saudi claims to the Buraimi Oasis which was owned by Muscat. But in the matter of Syria some degree of cooperation began to seem possible, with the organizing, perhaps in association with Iraq, of a pro-Western coup on the agenda. But most importantly, Lloyd and Dulles, meeting in Paris early in May, decided to let the Aswan High Dam project 'wither on the vine'.[10]

The American Administration, as the principal financial sponsor, obviously had the decisive voice about whether to proceed with the Aswan project. And at the time of Lloyd's meeting with Dulles the main reason for inclining against it was that Congressional approval was beginning to appear increasingly unlikely and the Administration naturally did not relish the prospect of a public rebuff. But on 16 May Dulles was further alienated by Egypt's decision to open diplomatic relations with Communist China, which the United States until the days of President Richard Nixon declined to recognize.

Gradually, it became clear to the British that Nasser would not be receiving the finance for the Dam from the United States. And Eden and Lloyd at any rate by no means regretted this in principle and took no steps to try to dissuade the Americans or to encourage other means of raising the money involving, for example, the West Europeans. Indeed, Eden was later to express anger when he heard that the British Board of Trade had been exploring this latter possibility. The only question for Eden and Lloyd was whether Nasser should be bluntly told that Anglo-American support for the Dam had been withdrawn. For there was an alternative possibility, namely that the Egyptians would continue indefinitely to haggle over the terms, concerning which, naturally, the Americans were now in no mood to make concessions.

The question was answered for Eden and Lloyd when the Egyptians, who had probably become aware through intelligence sources of the essence of the decision to allow the project to 'wither on the vine', decided in July to end the haggling. They suddenly withdrew all objections to the terms currently on offer and sought to bring matters to a head. Ahmed Hussein, the Egyptian Ambassador in Washington, accordingly requested an interview with Dulles on 19 July (mere days after the last British forces left the Canal Zone under the 1954 Agreement). The Ambassador asked for a straightforward 'yes' or 'no'. Dulles, apparently with no particular discourtesy, answered that the offer was withdrawn. Great Britain announced an identical decision on the following day.

Apparently expecting this answer, Nasser now sought his revenge and the hapless British, rather than the Americans, were to be the victims. Eden's 'authorized' biographer, Rhodes James, has seen fit to argue that some responsibility for this can be placed at Dulles's door: 'Nasser may well have planned what then happened, but it was the manner of the American decision that gave him the opportunity to describe this as a deliberate humiliation to himself and his country.'[11] Yet what alternative did Dulles have? The fact was that the policy of allowing the Dam project to 'wither on the vine' could no longer be sustained once the Egyptians had expressed unequivocal willingness to accept the terms on offer. At best, Dulles could only have stalled for a few more days or possibly weeks – with no obvious benefit to anyone.

As for Eden, his alleged reaction to the news of Dulles's meeting with Ambassador Hussein has been recorded by his Press Secretary, William Clark (who was later to resign in protest at the eventual Anglo-French invasion of Egypt):

This came through, as messages tended to, on the Reuters tape before it came through on the Foreign Office tape. I took it up, always glad to get credit for the press, to the Prime Minister in his bedroom. His comment was, 'Oh good, oh good for Foster. I didn't really think he had it in him.' Then there was a pause and, 'I wish he hadn't done it quite so abruptly.'[12]

Notes

1 Mohammed Heikal, *Nasser: the Cairo Documents* (London, 1972), p. 81.
2 Harold Macmillan, *Tides of Fortune, 1945–1955* (London, 1969), p. 634.
3 Quoted in Richard Lamb, *The Failure of the Eden Government* (London, 1987), p. 174.
4 Cab. 128/29, PRO.
5 Winthrop Aldrich Recollections, John Foster Dulles Oral History Collection, Princeton University Library, quoted in David Carlton, *Anthony Eden: a Biography* (London, 1981), p. 391.
6 Anthony Nutting quoted in Brian Lapping, *The End of Empire* (London, 1985), pp. 261–2. In his own earlier account Nutting attributed the word 'destroyed' rather than 'murdered' to Eden: Anthony Nutting, *No End of a Lesson: the Story of Suez* (London, 1967), p. 34.
7 Robert Rhodes James, *Anthony Eden* (London, 1986), p. 431.
8 Quoted in Lamb, *The Failure of the Eden Government*, pp. 189–90. Rhodes James published neither this nor other relevant telegrams, describing them coyly as 'remaining sensitive' (Rhodes James, *Anthony Eden*, p. 431).
9 Selwyn Lloyd, *Suez 1956: a Personal Account* (London, 1978), pp. 59–60.
10 Ibid., p. 69.
11 Rhodes James, *Anthony Eden*, p. 451.
12 Quoted in Lapping, *The End of Empire*, p. 262.

3 The Canal Nationalization Crisis

Egypt's coup: the immediate reaction

On 26 July 1956 Eden was host at a dinner at 10 Downing Street in honour of King Feisal of Iraq and his Prime Minister, Nuri es-Said. While at table the assembled company received the news that Nasser, during the course of a rabble-rousing speech in Alexandria, had proclaimed the nationalization of the Suez Canal hitherto owned by the Anglo-French Suez Canal Company. Dismay among the British and the Iraqis was general. Eden accordingly held an immediate post-prandial meeting with three of the four British Chiefs of Staff and with the French Ambassador and the American chargé d'affaires. There was heady talk of a rapid military response and the Chiefs were duly asked to produce appropriate plans as a matter of urgency.

Next day the British Cabinet met in formal session and heard the Chiefs state that nothing of a military nature could be done quickly. No mere airborne landings could be contemplated given the wartime precedents provided by Crete and Arnhem where casualties had been severe. So three divisions would have to be raised and an armada and air support would have to be assembled in the Eastern Mediterranean. All this would inevitably take many weeks.

It is usually assumed that Eden, disappointed at these tidings, reluctantly fell back, very much as a second best, on a policy of proposing in the interim, while the armada was being made ready, to engage in prolonged diplomatic discussions with other interested countries and, above all, with both France and the United States. But if more rapid military action had been possible was it really the case that the British Prime Minister would have simply issued an ultimatum (or something like it) to Egypt without further ado? Some scepticism may be in order, particularly if one considers the contrast with the way in which Margaret Thatcher's Cabinet handled the Argentinian seizure of the Falkland Islands in 1982. On that occasion, too, no immediate military response was physically available – and could not be so for many weeks. But it was made apparent to the world from the outset that force would be used if the Argentinians did not withdraw their troops. True, during the intervening weeks, diplomatic discussions were held but the British intention to use force if necessary was never in doubt.

In 1956 such absolute clarity about British intentions was conspicuously absent. Why? It surely was not because military force was not immediately available. Nor was it because the Canal, unlike the Falklands, was jointly owned with another nation, namely the French. For in Paris there would have been full and instant agreement with any British proposal for presenting an immediate ultimatum to Cairo. Nor was it because of doubts about the international legal aspect of the matter. For Eden from the outset carried his Cabinet (see Appendix II) for the proposition that the issue should not be looked at in those terms (though later the Lord Chancellor produced some dubious but essentially irrelevant arguments to the effect that Egypt had broken international law and that British military action could accordingly be held to be self-defence). The real reason for the contrast with 1982 was simply that Eden failed to show the same decisiveness as Thatcher at the outset of the crisis.

Eden's initial *privately expressed* desire at the end of July to use force, unilaterally if necessary, to reverse Nasser's seizure of the Canal is of course undoubted. Indeed, on 30 July at a meeting of the Egypt Committee (an inner Cabinet set up that day to manage the crisis) the Prime Minister and his closest advisers agreed that their aim should not just be settling their Canal grievance but the removal from power of Nasser himself. The relevant passage of the Minutes reads:

While our ultimate purpose was to place the Canal under international control, our immediate objective was to bring about the down fall of the present Egyptian Government. This might perhaps be achieved by less elaborate operations than those required to secure physical possession of the Canal itself. On the other hand it was argued that our case before world opinion was based on the need to secure international control over the Canal.[1]

All the same, this was not and never became a publicly proclaimed set of objectives, in contrast to the early posture of the Thatcher government in 1982 when a clear and simple line on aims and means was made known to the world. Some will judge that the ambiguity in 1956 arose because Eden was just too indecisive to issue an ultimatum in the wake of the nationalization of the Canal. Eager to wound, was he ultimately afraid to strike? After all, as has been seen, he had originally threatened behind closed doors and in secret despatches to punish King Hussein of Jordan in March 1956 for dismissing Glubb; and, if Nutting is to be believed, had spoken at that time of having Nasser murdered. But he had presently cooled down and recognized the case for avoiding drastic unilateral British punitive action over what in the view of the international community was a relatively minor provocation. Could it be, then, that Eden was no less guilty of bluster in his first private reaction to the Canal nationalization coup but that he almost immediately began to backslide?

Those attracted to this interpretation may find some confirmation in the line on Eden allegedly taken by Nasser when he finally decided to risk twisting the lion's tail. According to his confidant, Heikal, Nasser held that:

Eden was weak – weak in character, weak in his position in his party and government, and weak in his standing in the country. Eden was attracted by the idea of doing something violent. All the more so because he could probably count on the support of public opinion at home as well as on the American government, which would bitterly resent a slap in the face administered to its second most prominent member, Secretary of State John Foster Dulles.

But if he was to take advantage of these favourable circumstances Eden would have to act very quickly. The period of maximum danger for Egypt, Nasser believed, would be in the first few days after the nationalisation of the Suez Canal Company had been proclaimed. He thought that up to, say, August 10 there would be a 90 per cent risk of an armed attack on Egypt; for the rest of August the risk would decline to about 80 per cent; in September it would be down to 60 per cent; in the first half of October to 40 per cent; in the second half to 20 per cent and thereafter, thanks to the mobilisation of world opinion which Nasser confidently expected, the risk would virtually evaporate.[2]

Another broad interpretation of the contrast between 1956 and 1982, however, would lay less stress on Eden's personal indecisiveness and would instead focus on the importance of the 'special relationship' with the United States for the whole British policy-making elite during both the Suez and Falklands crises. In 1982 the unambiguous nature of the Argentinian act of aggression against the Falklands meant that there was never any likelihood that the United States would condemn out of hand the kind of recourse to force that the Thatcher government made plain from the outset was inevitable if Argentina did not back down. All that was in doubt was the extent of the American moral and material assistance that would be on offer. In 1956, by contrast, there was considerable doubt from the outset about what attitude the Americans would take towards even the basic proposition that the British and French had suffered such a blow at Egyptian hands that their use of force would be justified even as a last resort. Certainly nobody in Eden's Cabinet could plausibly have claimed in the days following Nasser's coup that the immediate despatch of an ultimatum to Cairo would have been acceptable to the United States. Hence the real choice at that point was between a policy of going ahead with such an ultimatum in any case – something the French would almost certainly have welcomed – or one of merely making military preparations while seeking to win over the Americans to at least acquiescing in the despatch of such an ultimatum at a later date. In spite of all the robust language behind closed doors, the latter broad choice was the one favoured by Eden and all his principal colleagues. What was to happen if the Americans could not be won over to such acquiescence, however, seems not to have been adequately addressed in the early stages of the crisis. The Cabinet Minutes for 27 July are revealing in this connection:

The Prime Minister said that ... the Cabinet must decide what our policy must be ... It must now be our aim to place the Suez Canal under the control of the Powers interested in international shipping and trade by means of a new international Commission on which Egypt would be given suitable representation ... The fundamental question before the Cabinet, however, was whether they were prepared in the last resort to pursue their objective by threat or even the use of force, and whether they were ready, in default of assistance from the United States and France, to take military action alone.

The Cabinet agreed that our essential interests in this area must, if necessary, be safeguarded by military action ...[3]

What, then, was simply not faced up to was that it might not just be a case of 'default of assistance from the United States' but outright opposition.

The initial signals from Washington were rather ambiguous on this crucial point, but we now know that Eisenhower soon absolutely set his face against any kind of military response to Nasser's coup. The only possible dispute is about the stage at which this did or should have become reasonably apparent to Eden and his colleagues.

On 27 July, the day following the coup, Eden sent Eisenhower a telegram in which he stated: 'My colleagues and I are convinced that we must be ready, in the last resort, to use force to bring Nasser to his senses. For our part we are prepared to do so. I have this morning instructed our Chiefs of Staff to prepare a military plan accordingly.' But the reference to 'last resort' seemed to Eisenhower to leave open the door to a possible diplomatic solution. This may have been reinforced by Eden's having added: 'However, the first step must be for you and us and France to exchange views, align our policies and concert together how we can best bring the maximum pressure to bear on the Egyptian Government.'[4] Certainly, Eisenhower was not sufficiently alarmed immediately to recall Dulles who was on a visit to Peru. Instead, he despatched Robert Murphy, Deputy Under-Secretary in the US State Department, to London to explore the situation. Murphy's reports of his conversations there on 29 and 30 July proved something of a turning point. For he conveyed verbal messages to the President indicating that both Eden and Macmillan were, after all, on the point of taking immediate military action. Murphy was probably deliberately misled, particularly by Macmillan who throughout the crisis pursued an erratic and ultimately self-serving course. At all events, Eisenhower took fright and decided to send Dulles to London to restrain the supposedly impetuous British.

The President drafted a personal letter for Dulles to hand to Eden on his arrival on 31 July. The full text (reproduced in Appendix I) shows that he was already taking a clear line against any immediate ultimatum to Egypt and was urging the convening of an international conference of interested parties.[5] In his memoirs Eden commented on this letter: 'The President did not rule out the use of force.'[6] But even his sympathetic 'authorized' biographer, Rhodes James, felt obliged to pass this critical judgement: 'This is technically true, but the whole tenor of the letter was in the opposite direction, and was confirmed by Dulles, who added his own comment on Eisenhower's letter, writing to Eden that it "refers not to going through the motions of having an intermediate conference but to the use of intermediate steps as a genuine and sincere effort to settle the problem and avoid the use of force".'[7] Rhodes James proceeds, however, to make the best case he can for his subject by claiming that Dulles signalled his personal divergence from Eisenhower on a number of occasions, thereby in large part causing the resulting alleged fatal misunderstandings between Great Britain and the United States. He wrote of Dulles:

[His] personal loathing of Nasser was manifest in his discussion with the British. He was definitely *not* his Master's Voice . . . The British in London, in spite of all [Sir Roger] Makins [British Ambassador in Washington] told them of the reality, genuinely believed that Dulles ran American foreign policy, with a somewhat lazy and uninvolved President somewhere in the background, who would, if it came to the crunch, support his old wartime allies and friends.[8]

This interpretation is unlikely to gain wide support. For the fact is that some in London did take extremely seriously various indications of Eisenhower's hostility to the use of force over the nationalization issue. And others, including perhaps Eden himself on occasions, wondered whether Dulles's views really diverged much from those of his chief, at any rate on the Canal issue.

The fact was that Dulles had a maddening habit of blowing hot and cold throughout the crisis. But this probably did not spring from genuine confusion or indecision on his part but from a desire, if possible, to gain time to allow calmer councils to prevail in London once the initial shock of Nasser's coup has begun to wear off. One of his aides, Robert Bowie, later explained Dulles's line as follows:

He did not really want to say explicitly that the use of force was out. He wanted to keep this as a possible threat to Nasser – as a sort of danger which Nasser couldn't rule out – that he had to take account of – hoping that this might bring him to make a deal on terms that would be mutually satisfactory. But Eden kept using this as a device for trying to force Dulles to say that force would be used . . . it was a sort of cat and mouse game, in which Dulles was constantly trying to maneuver the situation so that force wouldn't have to be used and that still a satisfactory solution could have been gotten. Eden was trying to maneuver the situation in such a way that the use of force would be legitimate, justified.[9]

Thus at his meeting with British and French leaders on 1 and 2 August Dulles urged that a maritime conference of Canal users be called and used much robust language about Nasser. In particular, Dulles stated that 'a way had to be found to make Nasser disgorge, what he was attempting to swallow', words which Eden claimed 'rang in his ears for months'[10] and which allegedly led the British to accept the idea of a conference. The French then reluctantly went along and an announcement was duly made on 3 August. But, though anti-Nasser, Dulles insisted that the conference could not begin before 16 August (a much later date than the British and French preferred) and, as already noted, he stressed in a comment on Eisenhower's letter that it 'refers [to] a genuine and sincere effort to settle the problem and avoid the use of force'.[11]

At a crucial full Cabinet meeting on 1 August the British decided to accept the conference suggestion.[12] Was this because Eden persuaded them to give Dulles the benefit of the doubt on the basis of private conversations? Or was it that the Cabinet instinctively recognized that an outright break with

Washington over the Canal issue was really not practical politics for a country whose national security policies had for so long been closely intermeshed with those of the United States? At all events, if ever there was a moment for the Cabinet to clarify in their own minds whether at the geo-political level Great Britain was in the last resort an auxiliary of the United States it was surely this. But Eden, consciously or not, obfuscated the point by permitting the Cabinet to move in two different directions at once. By agreeing to the American-led conference he in effect lost the chance to rally the nation behind a straightforward Anglo-French ultimatum to Egypt over the issue of the nationalization of the Canal. Other acceptable outcomes might, of course, later have emerged – for example, an Egyptian climbdown in the face of American-led diplomatic pressure or an American-approved military campaign against Egypt if Nasser took further provocative steps such as physically closing the Canal – but a 'straight bash' (as one Minister termed it) in response to the coup of 26 July was simply just not going to happen now that Dulles had successfully taken the British and the French in tow. Yet the thrust of this British policy decision was con-tradicted by Eden's failure in the ensuing days to prevent the gradual acceptance of military preparations – some made public and some ordered behind closed doors – that had the effect of raising expectations that a 'straight bash' was indeed a near-certainty if Nasser did not agree to a humiliating climbdown.

The weeks of indecision

So far as most backbenchers and the general public were concerned, the build-up of tension was symbolized by the announcement of the call-up of reservists on 2 August and by subsequent rumours of unusual movements of armed forces to British ports and subsequently to the Mediterranean theatre. At the same time many British Ministers and MPs made proclamations of such bellicosity as to suggest that a peaceful

outcome was improbable. In a Parliamentary debate on
2 August, for example, even the Labour Party appeared to be
in robust mood, with its leader Hugh Gaitskell comparing
Nasser to Hitler and Mussolini. Much of the press, too, took
an extremely jingoistic line and was not discouraged from
doing so by the government. It was of course possible that
some Ministers saw all this not as preparation for a nearly
inevitable war but as a necessary show of national resolve that
would influence both the Americans and the Egyptians in the
direction of a peaceful diplomatic outcome. But the minutes of
the crucial Egypt Committee, though at times ambiguous,
suggest that Eden and most of his principal lieutenants would
at this stage have been disappointed at any result that did not
end once and for all the threat to British interests posed by
Nasser – an unlikely outcome without at least some show of
force.

The military planning behind closed doors revealed the
same reluctance to recognize that agreeing to Dulles's conference proposal had sold the pass so far as a 'straight bash'
over the Canal coup was concerned. Conversations among
British and French military leaders proceeded early in August
as if Dulles and the maritime conference were simply an
irrelevance. And of the two main war aims priority was even
given to the more ambitious. The outcome was that the Chiefs
of Staff presented a plan code-named 'Musketeer' to the Egypt
Committee on 10 August. It envisaged a straightforward
assault on Egypt centred on Alexandria and obviously having
as its purpose the toppling of the Nasser regime. The alternative, at this stage deliberately eschewed, would have involved
landings at Port Said, thus permitting concentration on the
more modest goal of securing the Suez Canal. Eden, under
strong pressure from Macmillan, led his colleagues in accepting the former option. Even more important, an optimum date
of 15 September was fixed for landings in Alexandria and
preparations were put in hand, involving British reservists, that
could not in the nature of things be 'placed on hold' for an
indefinite period. (The worsening weather conditions in the
Eastern Mediterranean expected by mid-November were also
a factor.)

Yet on the previous day the same Egypt Committee had shown signs of at last beginning to grasp that the political initiative had been lost. The minutes for 9 August state:

They recognised that very difficult problems of timing were involved. Some diplomatic exchanges with the Egyptian Government would have to be carried through after the end of the conference . . . Although we should be unwilling to allow them to be unduly protracted, we might be liable to lose the support of other Powers if we appeared to be unwilling to entertain any reasonable counter-proposals which the Egyptian Government might make . . .

Similar difficulties would arise in connection with the summoning of Parliament . . . It would be highly embarrassing, to say the least, to have to invite Parliament to approve a proposal to launch a military operation against Egypt. If the issue were put to Parliament at that stage, such division of opinion as there was in the country would tend to be accentuated. It would not be easy for the Government to proceed with their intentions on the basis of a relatively narrow majority in a division in the House of Commons . . .

These considerations seemed to point to the conclusion that any military action against Egypt should be launched in retaliation against some aggressive or provocative act by the Egyptians.[13]

The British government thus found itself in a schizophrenic position. It had a military plan which was time-limited and which, by focusing on Alexandria, took no account whatever of world opinion. On the other hand, it was increasingly recognizing at the political level that a military operation was dependent on 'some aggressive or provocative act by the Egyptians' (that is, something additional to the coup of 26 July). Thus the conclusion seems to follow that if Nasser kept his head the British and French would be faced by mid-November at the latest with the need to order a humiliating stand-down for the forces assembled for 'Musketeer'.

Eden for his part seems not to have grasped this point with any clarity. Or perhaps he did and was simply taking a colossal gamble on a blunder by Nasser because he could see no superior alternative. If Eden was indeed at this stage driven consciously to take such risks it seems a fair inference that either his personal position or, alternatively, his assessment of his country's plight must have seemed to him to be nothing less than desperate. Could he have had any reasonable grounds for taking such a gloomy view? That he *appeared* to think the nationalization of the Canal was a supreme test for his country's future is undoubted, as his letters, his statements behind closed doors to colleagues and even his public pronouncements all bear witness. And he was given to drawing analogies with what had happened in the 1930s and, in particular, with the handling of the crisis over Hitler's remilitarization of the Rhineland in 1936 (about which he himself as the then Foreign Secretary may have had a bad conscience). The most striking exposition of his supposedly apocalyptic vision over Suez came in a letter to Eisenhower dated 6 September (reproduced in Appendix I) in which he discerned a plan designed by Nasser 'to expel all Western influence and interests from Arab countries' and eventually to deny oil to Western Europe after which 'we here shall all be at his mercy'. 'It would be an ignoble end to our long history', he concluded, 'if we tamely accepted to perish by degrees.'[14] But whether these opinions about the extent of Nasser's menace were really the principal motive in determining Eden's conduct is open to doubt.

It is right to state, however, that extreme assessments of what was at stake in the autumn of 1956 were then widely held in Great Britain. Much of the popular press, for example, makes extraordinary reading with the hindsight of more than three decades. And so does a perusal of the speeches of many Conservative MPs, and not only members of the 'Suez Group'. And even among Eden's closest associates in the Cabinet apocalyptic views were clearly held. Lord Home (later Sir Alec Douglas-Home), then Commonwealth Secretary, wrote privately to Eden on 24 August: 'I am convinced that we are finished if the Middle East goes and Russia and India and China rule from Africa to the Pacific.'[15] On the same day Alan Lennox-Boyd, the Colonial Secretary, wrote to the Prime Minister that 'if Nasser wins, or even appears to win we might . . . as well, as a government (and indeed a country) go out of business.'[16] As for Macmillan, his tone at the outset of the Crisis caused even Foreign Secretary Lloyd, a 'hawk' where Nasser was concerned, to write of his 'intemperate talk'.[17] He is said to have declared that 'Britain would not become another Netherlands' to Murphy. And, according to his own account, he told Dulles on 1 August 'as plainly as I could that we just could not afford to lose this game. It was a question not of honour only but survival.'[18]

Among Permanent Officials, too, extreme statements were not unknown (though less common than among politicians). In particular, Kirkpatrick, the Head of the Foreign Office, became a wild apocalyptic over the nationalization of the Canal. Shuckburgh referred in his diary entry for 24 September to a conversation with him:

Never have I heard such black pessimism. Set off by some mild criticism I made of the PM's handling of the Suez crisis, he said the PM was the only man in England who wanted the nation to survive; that all the rest of us have lost the will to live; that in two years' time Nasser will have deprived us of our oil, the sterling area fallen apart, no European defence possible, unemployment and unrest in the UK and our standard of living reduced to that of the Yugoslavs or Egyptians.[19]

A degree of hyperbole may have crept into all these statements, and in the case of Macmillan we may be dealing with nothing more than the cynical machinations of an opportunist intent on creating conditions in which he might have a chance to seize the premiership. But the various statements did reflect something of the British *Zeitgeist* and it is thus not unlikely that in such a context Eden, too, really meant a large part of what he said and wrote about the coup of July 1956. On the other hand, nobody becomes a British Prime Minister without possessing acute instincts for political survival. Hence historians are entitled to wonder whether Eden failed to overcome his phobia about Nasser and to give sufficient weight to Eisenhower's powerful counter-arguments essentially for reasons of personal political calculation. For the fact was that a repetition in the Suez context of his conduct over the Glubb Affair – initial rage followed by cooler second thoughts – might well have been fatal to his entire authority. It may be therefore that his approach throughout August and September 1956 appears in retrospect to be schizophrenic for no other reason than that he could not clearly see whether ultimate acquiescence in or eventual resistance to Nasser's coup was the more hazardous personal course. And, of course, as noted earlier, something might have turned up to resolve his dilemma – above all, the Americans might have had a change of heart in the event of some further outrage by Nasser.

At all events, August and September were to be months of drift rather than decisiveness. The Conference of Maritime Nations duly met between 16 and 23 August at Lancaster House in London. Of the 22 nations present, 18 (India, Indonesia, the Soviet Union and Ceylon being the exceptions) subscribed to a resolution promoted by a vigorous-sounding Dulles. This in effect called upon Egypt to accept that the Canal should be run by an international board and that it should not be closed to any user for political reasons. A five-man mission, headed by Australian Premier Robert Menzies, was despatched to Cairo to try to convert Nasser to this plan but was met with a stubborn negative.

Eden later implied that he had been so impressed by Dulles's language at the Lancaster House Conference that he had been led to expect an understanding American attitude if the British and French saw fit to react with force should the Menzies mission fail. But, if so, he was deceiving himself. For while Menzies was actually in Cairo Eisenhower publicly stated that the United States was 'committed to a peaceful settlement of the dispute, nothing else'.[20] And Dulles soon made it privately clear to the British and the French that he did not favour early referral of the dispute to the United Nations Security Council and that if such referral did take place as a mere prelude to an ultimatum to Egypt no American support in the Security Council could be counted on.

What Dulles now recommended to the British, on 4 September, was the convening of another international conference in London. On 11 September, after prolonged agonizing and in the face of French disapproval, Eden's Cabinet agreed to this proposal (see Appendix II). A conference of 18 nations duly met between 19 and 21 September and set up a body known as the Suez Canal Users' Association (SCUA). But its impact on Nasser was destined to be negligible. Indeed, as early as

12 September, just after the calling of the conference had been announced in London and Washington, its worth was decisively undermined by Dulles's public statement that so far as the Suez Canal was concerned 'We [the United States] do not intend to shoot our way through.' And on 2 October he reinforced this statement by saying at a press conference of SCUA: 'There is talk of teeth being pulled out of the plan, but I know of no teeth: there were no teeth in it, so far as I am aware.'[21]

These remarks have been repeatedly used by apologists for the British government as evidence of Dulles's essential hostility to British aims. And there clearly is a case to be made along such lines. It sits badly, however, with the interpretation advanced by Eden's 'authorized' biographer, Rhodes James, namely that the British had grounds for seeing Dulles as potentially more sympathetic than Eisenhower to the use of force to resolve the Canal dispute. At all events, Eden and his principal colleagues must have been very obtuse indeed if they really believed that agreeing to the SCUA proposal was bringing nearer the day when an ultimatum to Nasser could be issued with at least tacit American approval. For, apart from Dulles's public statements, Eden had by now received several further letters from Eisenhower (see Appendix I) unmistakably setting his face against the use of force unless Nasser gave further provocation.

Yet in his memoirs Lloyd felt able to write of Dulles's performance at the SCUA Conference: 'I do not think that anyone who listened to him could have felt that if Nasser rejected the SCUA plan, and if the Security Council failed to obtain a solution, Dulles would do other than accept the use of force, even if the United States did not take part.'[22] This echoed Eden's own later declaratory line. And, according to Rhodes James, 'Eden subsequently – and indeed for the rest of his life – considered that his acceptance of SCUA was the greatest mistake of his career, for which he reproached himself greatly.'[23] More than a dash of scepticism about this approach may, however, be in order. For while neither Eden nor Lloyd was among the cleverest men to hold high office in Great Britain, they were not total fools. And evidence in the contemporary records suggests that the SCUA proposal was accepted *without* major illusions about American intentions. The fact was that there was really no practical alternative.

At all events, at least two senior actors, one in Paris and one in London, reached the conclusion at this time that a war simply over the nationalization of the Canal was no longer likely. General Paul Ely, Chief of Staff of the French Armed Forces, recalled that 'the Suez affair seemed to me personally as very probably buried and I had the feeling that any military intervention was no longer to be expected.'[24] Likewise even Nutting (who otherwise did much to create the image of Eden as an unalterably single-minded fanatic on the subject of Nasser) later wrote that 'Eden could not at this juncture see how it would be possible to use force unless Nasser struck the first blow.'[25] What these statements confirm was that Eden had had to recognize emerging evidence that support for a 'straight bash' over the Canal issue had ebbed sufficiently to make it an extremely hazardous project indeed. And the American factor, thought extremely important, was by no means all that pointed towards caution.

For example, Gaitskell, after his initial expressions of indignation, was increasingly stressing in response to left-wing pressures the need to secure Security Council approval for any military action. This, while not a complete contradiction of his original line, constituted a distinct shift of emphasis which presaged the country going to war, if at all, with the House of Commons divided on party lines as had not of course been the case in the two world wars or in the Korean War.

Moreover, the political nation as a whole was likely to have been similarly split. For, as already noted, this was an era in which many *bien pensants* in all parties were still optimistic about building international institutions and strengthening the rule of law in international relations. The United Nations in 1956 was not seen – rightly so – in the same jaundiced way that is nowadays widespread in the West. For the Soviet bloc was usually isolated at New York. And the Third World members, one year after the Bandung Conference, were still relatively small in number and much less virulently anti-Western than they are today. In short, to take military action in defiance of the

United Nations was not something to be lightly attempted in the moral climate of 1956. This was particularly the case, of course, so far as many members of the 'chattering class' as distinct from the 'working class' were concerned.

It was also apparent that the Commonwealth would be bitterly divided by a recourse to force. Australia and New Zealand might have been supportive, but even in their cases much might have turned on the extent of American pressure in the opposite direction. But the rest of the major nations of the Commonwealth would assuredly have been in varying degrees hostile, with India leading the pro-Nasser force in the New Commonwealth, and with Canada certain to support the United States.

What was probably decisive, however, in leading Eden to accept the SCUA proposal was that by early September even his own Cabinet had begun to show signs of being unsustainably divided on the matter of a 'straight bash' on the Canal issue. The leader of the 'doves' was Sir Walter Monckton, who served as Minister of Defence during the first phase of the Crisis. He spoke with particular vigour on 24 August at a meeting of the Egypt Committee, provoking angry letters to the Prime Minister from Home and Lennox-Boyd. He restated his doubts at a full Cabinet on 28 August (see Appendix II). Then, on 10 September, he circulated to the Cabinet a paper from the Chiefs of Staff urging the abandonment of the original 'Musketeer' aim of landings in Alexandria. Instead, apparently for a mix of military and political reasons, it was held that contingency planning should focus on Port Said. Monckton added his own gloss to the Chiefs' proposal: 'It is therefore of the greatest importance that this invasion of Egypt is launched with our moral cause unassailable and the start of the war clearly and definitely Nasser's responsibility and no one else's.' Eden, while angered at the *volte face* by the Chiefs, did not feel able to overrule them and hence 'Musketeer Revise' was endorsed by the Egyptian Committee and forced on the despairing French.[26] Thus strengthened, Monckton went even further at a full Cabinet on the following day, 11 September, when he declared that 'Any premature recourse to force, especially without the support and approval of the United

States, was likely to precipitate disorder throughout the Middle East and to alienate a substantial body of public opinion in this country and elsewhere throughout the world.'[27] His was certainly not the majority view but Eden had to reckon with the possibility that if at this late stage he sought support for a 'straight bash' over the nationalization of the Canal Monckton might be backed by several other Cabinet Ministers who were thought to be uneasy but who had thus far kept a low profile. In particular, R. A. Butler, the Leader of the House and Lord Privy Seal, had shown no enthusiasm for the more 'hawkish' counsels and had emerged as a supporter of the case for making a *sincere* reference to the Security Council before any use of force could be contemplated.

On the 'hawkish' side of the argument the uncontested leader was, of course, Macmillan. As has been seen, he was from the outset far more extreme than either Eden or Lloyd. As one Cabinet Minister later put it, the Chancellor of the Exchequer 'was excessively vehement about military action from the very beginning, virtually regardless of the consequences or the methods'.[28] He was, however, by no means isolated. For probably a majority of the Cabinet were in varying degrees nearer to his position than to that of Monckton.

All this meant that Eden could easily find himself facing resignation threats from one side or the other and perhaps both in the event that he proposed any really decisive action. And this may have been the pre-eminent reason why no such decisive action was actually taken during August and September and why British policy had an essentially schizophrenic character symbolized by robust military preparations proceeding while on the diplomatic front something approaching 'appeasement' was in evidence.

Reference to the Security Council: the 'six principles'

With the end of the SCUA Conference Eden was, however, beginning to run out of options. But he had still one more card to play before the noose tightened around his neck. This was to refer the dispute to the Security Council and see whether direct talks with Egypt in that forum would yield any results. Reference was accordingly made by Great Britain and a sceptical France on 23 September. Consideration of the issues began on 5 October and from 9 to 12 October Lloyd and Christian Pineau, the French Foreign Minister, engaged in direct negotiations with Mahmoud Fawzi, their Egyptian counterpart. Agreement was soon reached on the so-called 'six principles' for a settlement. These were:

1. There should be free and open transit through the Canal without discrimination, overt or covert.
2. The sovereignty of Egypt should be respected.
3. The operation of the Canal should be insulated from the politics of any country.
4. The manner of fixing tolls and charges should be decided by agreement between Egypt and the users.
5. A fair proportion of the dues should be allocated to development.
6. Unresolved disputes between the Suez Canal Company and Egypt should be settled by arbitration.

By mid-October the only remaining stumbling block, though possibly a substantial one, turned on the arrangements for supervising the implementation of the 'six principles'. All the same, both sides had travelled quite a distance towards a peaceful settlement, leading Eisenhower to say that 'it looks like here is a very great crisis that is behind us'.[29]

The central question is whether Eden and Lloyd were in earnest at this stage about desiring some kind of negotiated settlement. If so, it follows that the actual toppling of Nasser as a serious short-term British objective was being abandoned; and that even on the Canal issue a total climbdown by Egypt was no longer seen in London as a *sine qua non*. (For evidence on this point see Appendix II, 3 October 1956.) Many contemporaries, both 'hawks' and 'doves', concluded at the time that this was indeed the direction in which Eden and Lloyd were moving. Among them were the French leaders who naturally regretted the implications.

Recrimination between the British and French leaders had occurred as early as 26 September when Eden and Lloyd visited Paris. And Pineau, in particular, emerged as an un-reconstructed 'hawk'. Eden telegraphed this message to Butler in London:

My own feeling is that the French, particularly Pineau, are in a mood to blame everyone including us if military action is not taken by the end of October. They alleged that the weather would preclude it later. I contested that. [Guy] Mollet [The French Premier], as I believe, would like to get a settlement on reasonable terms if he could. I doubt whether Pineau wants a settlement at all.[30]

As Lloyd succinctly commented in his memoirs: 'This message also does not reveal undue bellicosity on Eden's part at that meeting.'[31] More evidence that during this phase Eden was basically leaning towards 'a settlement on reasonable terms' is provided by messages revealing concern at Pineau's initial intransigence at the UN talks and later relief at his apparent mellowing under pressure.[32]

warlike

Yet the appearance of a crisis petering out was nevertheless illusory. For the fundamental schizophrenia in British policy had still not been removed. In short, the Cabinet had yet to agree to reverse the military preparations and send the increasingly restive reservists back into civilian life. And Eden still could not bring himself, for whatever reason, to ask his colleagues to take this step – no matter how logical it seemed in the light of the obvious impossibility of now going to war over the nationalization of the Canal. In the first days of October, then, he was still hoping, with increasing desperation, for something to turn up. Suddenly, on the 14 October, it did: two French emissaries arrived at Chequers with what Nutting called 'an invitation to a conspiracy'.[33]

Notes

1 Cab. 134/1216, PRO.
2 Mohammed Heikal, *Cutting through the Lion's Tail: Suez through Egyptian Eyes* (London, 1986), p. 119.
3 Cab. 128/30, PRO. For a fuller version see Appendix II.

4 Eden to Eisenhower, 27 July 1956, Prem. 11/1177, PRO. For a fuller version see Appendix I.

5 Eisenhower to Eden, 31 July 1956; see Appendix I.

6 Anthony Eden, *Full Circle* (London, 1960), p. 436.

7 Robert Rhodes James, *Anthony Eden* (London, 1986), p. 473.

8 Ibid., p. 476.

9 Robert R. Bowie Recollections, Dulles Oral History Collection, Princeton University Library, quoted in David Carlton, *Anthony Eden: a Biography* (London, 1981), p. 413.

10 Eden, *Full Circle*, p. 437.

11 Rhodes James, *Anthony Eden*, p. 473.

12 Cab. 128/30, PRO.

13 Cab. 134/1216 (Confidential Annex), PRO.

14 Eden to Eisenhower, 6 September 1956, Prem. 11/1177, PRO; see Appendix I.

15 Home to Eden, 24 August 1956, quoted in Peter Hennessy, 'The scars of Suez', *The Listener*, 5 February 1987.

16 Lennox-Boyd to Eden, 24 August 1956, quoted in Hennessy, 'The scars of Suez'.

17 Selwyn Lloyd, *Suez 1956: a Personal Account* (London, 1978), p. 75.

18 Robert Murphy, *Diplomat among Warriors* (London, 1964), pp. 461–5; and Harold Macmillan, *Riding the Storm, 1956—1959* (London, 1971), p. 106.

19 Evelyn Shuckburgh, *Descent to Suez: Diaries 1951—56* (London, 1986), p. 360.

20 Lloyd, *Suez 1956*, p. 130.

21 Eden, *Full Circle*, p. 483; and Lloyd, *Suez 1956*, p. 152.

22 Lloyd, *Suez 1956*, p. 144.

23 Rhodes James, *Anthony Eden*, p. 512.

24 Quoted in Carlton, *Anthony Eden*, p. 420.

25 Anthony Nutting, *No End of a Lesson: the Story of Suez* (London, 1967), p. 63.

26 Cab. 134/1216, PRO. For further details see Richard Lamb, *The Failure of the Eden Government* (London, 1987), pp. 212–14. See also Anthony Gorst, 'A survey of Cabinet discussion: July–September 1956', *Contemporary Record*, vol. 1, no. 3 (autumn 1987).

27 Cab. 128/30, PRO. For a fuller version see Appendix II.

28 Quoted in Rhodes James, *Anthony Eden*, pp. 494–5.

29 Lloyd, *Suez 1956*, p. 160.

30 Ibid., p. 151.

31 Ibid.

32 For this point I am indebted to W. Scott Lucas, a doctoral candidate at the London School of Economics, who presented evidence to this effect at a seminar held on 1 July 1987 under the auspices of the Association of Contemporary Historians.

33 Nutting, *No End of a Lesson*, p. 90.

4 Conspiracy with France and Israel

Collusion

General Maurice Challe, a Deputy Chief of Staff of the French Air Force, and Albert Gazier, France's Minister of Labour deputizing for Pineau, arrived at Chequers on 14 October to be received by Eden (accompanied by Nutting). In his memoirs Challe wrote of Eden's demeanour in unflattering terms: 'His anxiety was to have the appearance of not being the aggressor. The general hypocrisy required that one prepared more or less lame pretexts. They deceived nobody but certain persons pretended to believe them. As if the confiscation of the Canal was not enough. Thus I presented the pretext or rather the scenario that he wanted.'[1]

The simple scenario that Challe so contemptuously presented was that Israel should in effect be encouraged to attack Egypt in such a way as to enable Great Britain and France to claim that the safety of the Canal was at risk and thus be able to send forces there to separate the combatants. What would happen thereafter was unclear. But the British and the French would at least have found a way to carry out the first stage of 'Musketeer Revise': the British reservists would not have to be stood down without seeing some action; and Egyptian prestige would have been to some extent punctured.

Nutting, who first revealed the story of the Chequers encounter in 1967, depicted Eden as having no reservations about how to respond. True, Eden did not formally commit himself, saying that he must first consult his colleagues. But

Nutting claimed that he 'knew then that, no matter what contrary advice he might receive over the next forty-eight hours, the Prime Minister had already made up his mind to go along with the French plan'.[2] This may be an over-simplification. For the fact is that Eden did not at this stage know what, if anything, would be required of the British by way of 'encouragement' to the Israelis to carry out their part in Challe's plan. A degree of mere contingency planning with the French would be one thing; plans based on definite foreknowledge of Israeli intentions something else; and a trilateral formal collusive deal something altogether different. The Chequers meeting, then, while a turning point of a kind, was *not* the occasion on which Eden made any irrevocable decisions.

All the same, it is probably fair to conclude that he was by now definitely predisposed to take seriously plans involving the Israelis. For he had just returned from the Conservative Party Conference, held in Llandudno, where the full magnitude of the domestic pressures on him had been strikingly apparent. A full-scale debate had taken place on 11 October during which anti-Egyptian feelings ran high. According to Leon D. Epstein:

The motion proposed by the leadership was little more than an endorsement of the government's efforts to reach 'a just solution'. It said nothing about military force and also nothing about the government's continued commitment to international control of the canal which had been the 'just solution' previously urged. It was this form of solution which, it was now plain, could be achieved only by force of arms against Egypt.

Nevertheless Captain Waterhouse, for the Suez Group, successfully proposed an addendum to the official resolution. Obviously so popular in the Conservative ranks that it had to be accepted by the leadership, the addendum put after 'just solution' the words 'designed to ensure international control of the canal in accordance with the proposals of the London Conference'. In this amended form, the motion was carried in the huge mass meeting with only one dissent. The meaning of the language of the addendum had been spelled out by its principal advocates, Waterhouse and Julian Amery. As Waterhouse said, in moving his addendum, '. . . at all costs and by all means Nasser's aggression must be resisted and defeated. For let us have no doubt at all, that at this moment Britain is at a vital cross roads in her history.' Let us tell the Prime Minister, he added, that if he will lead we will follow. Amery was more explicit. He told the party conference that the addendum would give the lie to 'all those rumours that we are abandoning the concept of control for the concept of supervision'. And if the current British appeal for control should fail in the United Nations Security Council, then 'our hands are free to use any and every measure that may be necessary to achieve our ends, including, if necessary, the use of force'. This Britain should do, Amery declared, if necessary even against American wishes. There was not much doubt that he thought it would be necessary.[3]

It had originally been intended that the reply for the government would be given by Lord Salisbury, the Lord President of the Council. But he was too ill to attend the Conference and accordingly Nutting was asked to deliver the speech for him. He agreed to do this and found himself reading out what he later characterized as 'a very combative piece of prose'.[4] Whether he found this as disagreeable as he later made out is a matter for dispute.[5] But it was undoubtedly well received. Then, on the last day of the Conference, 13 October, Eden himself addressed the delegates and made no effort to lower the temperature. On the contrary, he went out of his way to emphasize that the use of force against Egypt was not ruled out:

President Eisenhower in his press conference on Thursday is reported to have said that you must have peace with justice, or it is not peace. I agree with those words. We should all take them as our text. That is why we have always said that with us force is the last resort, but it cannot be excluded. Therefore, we have refused to say that in no circumstances would we ever use force. No responsible Government could ever give such a pledge.[6]

This passage was greeted with such great enthusiasm by the delegates that the Prime Minister must have realized that any compromise solution, such as Lloyd was working towards in New York, would be deeply unpopular in the Conservative Party. If, for example, Macmillan had seen fit to resign in protest at such a compromise, Eden could have been in no doubt about which of them would be the principal recipient of the cheers at the next Party Conference. And such was the apparent fanaticism of the 'Suez Group' of MPs that serious trouble for the government in Parliament in the more immediate future could also not be ruled out. All this serves to explain, even if it does not justify, Eden's anxiety to explore Challe's plan with the French at the earliest moment.

Following the departure of Challe and Gazier from Chequers on 14 October, Eden accordingly decided to summon Lloyd back from New York for urgent consultations. The latter arrived in London on the 16 October and, according to his own account, after a briefing from Nutting he at once joined a meeting of Ministers. No minutes of this meeting appear to have survived. According to Richard Lamb:

Nutting told the author that he remembers well the meeting of the Egypt Committee which took place at 10 Downing Street that morning. No record exists in the archives, and Eden must have ordered Norman Brook to expunge the minutes because the files show that the thirty-third meeting of the Egypt Committee took place on 10 October and the thirty-fourth on Wednesday, 17 October. (No Cabinet meeting, either, is recorded as taking place between 9 and 18 October.)

According to Nutting, on 16 October Butler was not present as he was conducting the Queen around the Calder Hall power station, but Antony Head, Monckton, Peter Thorneycroft [President of the Board of Trade] and Kilmuir were there as well as himself. Eden explained the plan for collusion with the French and Israelis which had been discussed at Chequers on the previous Sunday. Nutting says once again he protested vigorously; Monckton also protested, but with less vehemence. The rest of the Committee agreed with the Prime Minister, who said he would now tell the French Government that the plan would go ahead.[7]

If minutes really were expunged on Eden's orders it might be held to indicate that he was already committed to a course that he knew would be open to the charge of being essentially dishonourable. But on the point about expunging records an open verdict appears at the present to be the only safe one.

More prima facie evidence that Eden was aware that he was coming perilously close to the limits of what a statesman in a democracy can do is, however, apparent from his conduct later on the same day, 16 October. For, accompanied by a doubtless exhausted Lloyd, he flew without delay to Paris for a meeting with Mollet and Pineau from which all officials were pointedly excluded. Sir Gladwyn Jebb, the British Ambassador in Paris, subsequently sent a formal letter of protest to Lloyd, emphasizing the novel nature of this arrangement.[8]

For knowledge of what happened at the meeting of the four principals we are largely dependent on the testimony of Lloyd. Writing in his generally candid memoirs of the Suez Affair, he signally failed to confirm that there was any proposal at this stage for a formal tripartite conspiracy with Israel. Instead, the discussion appears to have centred on contingency planning. He wrote:

The French summed up our discussions by formulating two questions. In answer to the question whether we would fight to defend Nasser [if attacked by Israel], Eden said that he thought the answer was 'No'. As to the second question, whether we would intervene to safeguard the Canal and limit hostilities, he thought the answer was 'Yes', but he would have to obtain the approval of his Cabinet colleagues for both those answers.[9]

Eden and Lloyd clearly expected the French to take these answers as a British indication that they could inform the Israelis of the gist of the conversation. The French seemingly went further, however, and, according to Moshe Dayan, presented the Israelis with what they called a British plan:

The first paragraph stated that Britain and France would demand of both Egypt and Israel that they retire from the Canal area, and if one side refused, Anglo-French forces would intervene to ensure the smooth operation of the Canal. The purpose of this paragraph was to provide the legal, political, and moral justification for the invasion of Egypt by Britain and France. The second paragraph declared that the British would not go to the aid of Egypt if war broke out between her and Israel. But this was not the case as regards Jordan, with whom Britain had a valid defense treaty.[10]

Lloyd commented that if this is what the French said 'it was embroidered on the way beyond all recognition.'[11] Was this a fair comment on Lloyd's part? Might Eden have gone further with the French without telling his somewhat legalistic Foreign Secretary? We may never know.

One aspect of Dayan's account, however, is beyond question: the British were committed to the defence of Jordan and had wished the French to make this clear to the Israelis. Certainly, the Jordanian factor in the evolution of British policy should not be underrated. For what Eden and his colleagues, and particularly the Chiefs of Staff, had come to fear early in October 1956 was that they would indeed find themselves involved in war in the Middle East but against Israel not Egypt; or even against both at once. On 10 October, for example, Earl Mountbatten, the First Sea Lord, had told the Chiefs of Staff:

if during Musketeer Israel attacked Jordan and the United States went to Jordan's aid against Israel then we and the United States would be fighting on opposite sides. We should be the unwilling allies of Israel and our forces in Jordan would be hostages to fortune. If the United States had gone to the aid of Jordan and Egypt before Musketeer was launched, it would not then be practicable for us to launch Musketeer.[12]

Apprehension in London was heightened on that same day, 10 October, by a major Israeli raid into Jordanian territory at Qalqilya. How ironic, then, if the forces assembled to check or overthrow Nasser had had to be sent instead to support the British client-state of Jordan against a full-scale Israeli invasion, with Nasser cheering on the British against his ultimate enemy. Yet there was undeniably some risk that this would have been the outcome if the British had refused to give any kind of encouragement, direct or indirect, to the Israelis to attack Egypt rather than Jordan; and, above all, if the New York negotiations had culminated in a compromise solution to the Canal dispute. In short, here was a complicating factor which may have at least reinforced the willingness of Eden, Lloyd and others in London to succumb to the temptations on offer in Paris.

The threat to Jordan was certainly explored by the full British Cabinet at its seminal meeting of 18 October (see Appendix II). Eden indicated that the Israelis might be about to attack either Jordan or Egypt. He appears to have met with no opposition when making it clear that Great Britain would have to defend Jordan but that defending Egypt would be out of the question notwithstanding the obligation involved in the Tripartite Declaration of 1950 (which required Great Britain, France and the United States to come to the aid of either party to the Israeli–Egyptian dispute if subjected to invasion by the other). Eden added that it would be 'far better from our point of view' that Israel should attack Egypt rather than Jordan. He continued that the Cabinet should be aware that 'while we continued to seek an agreed settlement of the Suez dispute . . . it was possible that the issue might be brought more rapidly to a head as a result of military action by Israel against Egypt.'[13] In putting matters this way was Eden being less than candid with the Cabinet? The answer would appear to turn in large measure on whether one accepts Lloyd's account of what had occurred in the Paris meeting with Mollet and Pineau. If no formal Anglo-French plan was agreed in Paris for putting to the Israelis (as Lloyd maintained), then Eden would seem to have been reasonably straightforward with his colleagues. At all events, he carried them with him when he came to ask them what Great Britain would do if an Israeli advance into Egypt threatened the Canal. As Lloyd wrote shortly afterwards: '[Eden] said that it was his view that we must at all costs prevent fighting over the Canal, and damage to the Canal itself and shipping passing through it. He said that he had discussed this with some of his senior colleagues and they had agreed to this view. No one in the Cabinet disagreed.'[14]

The full concurrence of the colleagues was perhaps more apparent than real. For Monckton may be presumed to have had serious reservations, and Butler, according to his own account, had intervened to query the wisdom of planning an intervention to separate the combatants if the Canal was held to be menaced: 'I was impressed by the audacity of thinking behind this plan but concerned about the public reaction. I wondered whether an agreement with the French and the Israelis designed to free the Suez Canal and eventually to internationalize it, would not meet our objective.'[15] Up to this stage, however, Eden seemed to have a secure majority for his policy. In short, all that was now needed for him to be in sight of a victory against the odds was for the Israelis to attack Egypt without more ado. Had they been prepared to go ahead in these circumstances the chances are indeed that, whatever had subsequently occurred, Eden's reputation would now stand much higher than it does. For he would presumably have had to be found 'not guilty' of outright 'collusion' with Israel. And even the charge that he had 'foreknowledge' probably could not have been made to stick. For the fact was that as of 18 October, though he may have thought it probable, he actually did not know with certainty that Israel would attack Egypt.

The Israelis, however, declined to act without more ado. They decided to send Prime Minister David Ben-Gurion and several others to Paris for direct discussions. And they appear to have indicated to the French that a British representative would also have to go to Paris to give assurances as to precisely what action Great Britain proposed to take in the event of their invading Egypt. This news led Eden to convene a meeting at Chequers on 21 October. According to Lloyd, those present, apart from himself, were Butler, Macmillan, Antony Head (who had just succeeded Monckton as Minister of Defence), Kilmuir (probably), Norman Brook (the Secretary to the Cabinet), Richard Powell (Permanent Secretary at the Ministry of Defence) and General Charles Keightley (the Commander-in-Chief of 'Musketeer Revise').[16] The upshot was the astonishing decision that Lloyd should travel incognito to Paris on the next day, 22 October, to meet French and Israeli leaders. This was probably the most seminal move made by Eden and his colleagues throughout the entire Suez Crisis. For it meant that they were in effect prepared to enter into a direct tripartite conspiracy against Egypt. For the first time they had decided to run the risk that they might be sooner or later exposed as having engaged in an outright instigation of an Israeli attack on Egypt and that the operation ostensibly intended to separate the combatants in the Canal area would be seen as dishonourable and hypocritical by any standards. Such exposure has of course come about and has left Eden at least with a permanently sullied reputation. Even his 'authorized' biographer has written of Eden moving from 'an absolutely legitimate position to what was perilously close to being an illegitimate one'.[17]

Why did Eden cross this perfectly obvious if thin line? One writer on the Eden premiership has argued that health was a factor:

At that time Eden's health was not good. His doctors prescribed him amphetamines to buck him up when he felt tired, and barbiturates to help him sleep. Thirty years ago top physicians prescribed these dangerous drugs in a way which would shock modern practitioners. I am convinced that these drugs flawed his judgement during the three months of strain after the Suez Canal was nationalized.[18]

This is a defence Eden himself would have found more repugnant than many an attack. Yet the health argument is likely to receive wide future currency, together with variants on it that see him as either a victim of inherited mental instability or as someone whose mind had become essentially unhinged as a result of many personal tragedies and setbacks experienced earlier in his life (see chapter 1). Such speculations will always appeal to a certain kind of psycho-historian, but they are essentially unprovable.

In the case of Eden and the Suez Crisis, however, it is important to point out that the dishonourable conspiracy with France and Israel was *not* his sole responsibility. On the contrary, the idea had germinated in Paris. Yet there is no evidence that Mollet, Pineau and Challe were either physically or mentally ill. Again, the crucial decision to send Lloyd to meet the Israelis was *not* Eden's alone. It was at least acquiesced in by his three most senior colleagues, Macmillan, Butler and Lloyd, with the first still apparently at this stage a positive enthusiast for any kind of action against Nasser. But it has not been suggested that Macmillan also was ill or mad. In short, it seems the safer line for the historian is to presume that Eden, however unwise or dishonourable, did not lack apparently rational reasons for adopting the course he did.

It seems likely that domestic pressures, as already indicated, were pre-eminent for Eden. But we should not underestimate the Jordanian factor in influencing some of his colleagues to support him. For by chance the news from Amman on the eve of the Israelis' arrival in Paris was particularly alarming: the Jordanians had just elected a pro-Egyptian government. This, of course, made it much more likely that Jordan would be attacked by Israel and maybe also by Iraq.[19]

Lloyd, in particular, as his own account reveals, was deeply concerned that Great Britain's standing among moderate Arab states should not be seen to suffer as a result of indecisiveness. Yet the prospect of a crude deal with the Israelis clearly left him feeling uneasy. For should it 'leak' the damage likely to be done to his country's reputation among all Arabs, moderate or militant, was likely to be disastrous. Accordingly, on his arrival on 22 October in Sèvres, a suburb of Paris, he tried to keep the Israelis at arm's length. He saw his task as reassuring them that *if* they attacked Egypt in such a way as to menace the Canal Great Britain would join France in issuing an ultimatum to both countries requiring them to withdraw forces from the area of the Canal and to permit an Anglo-French policing operation. He gave the impression to the Israelis that he saw this as something less than an instigation to the Israelis to attack. And he later sent a letter to Pineau spelling out that this was indeed his line.[20] But if he really believed this, he was surely deceiving only himself. His very presence at Sèvres meant that his country was taking part in what, in plain words, can only be called a conspiracy to attack Egypt. But he indicated that the Israelis would have to attack first and realize that they would be recipients of an ultimatum from Great Britain and France. In short, the Israelis were in effect being invited to take steps that would lead them to receive an ultimatum threatening them with the use of force, as novel a manoeuvre as any seen in the entire history of modern international politics.

The Israelis evidently found Lloyd's hypocrisy too sanctimonious to take entirely seriously and gave no sign that they would proceed in the way envisaged. As Lloyd's Assistant Private Secretary, Donald Logan, who was present, wrote: 'He [Ben-Gurion] felt Israel was being asked to solve Britain's and France's problems by accepting the opprobrium of aggression, followed by the ignominy of accepting an ultimatum.'[21] Finally, however, Lloyd was asked to return to London to report to Eden and he was left in no doubt that in any event the Israelis would not move unless the British undertook to bomb Egyptian airfields at a very early stage in any hostilities.

On the following day, 23 October, the full Cabinet (see Appendix II) was told that: 'From secret conversations which had been held in Paris with representatives of the Israeli Government, it now appeared that the Israelis would not alone launch a full-scale attack against Egypt.'[22] What was not apparently made clear, however, was that Lloyd had personally met Ben-Gurion or that he had discussed terms on which Israel might attack Egypt. Thus, perhaps for the first time in the Suez Crisis, the Cabinet was being deceived on what appears to be a major point. Nevertheless, Eden did not conceal from his colleagues that he was still considering the case for going ahead with an Anglo-French assault on Egypt even in the absence of any Israeli action.[23]

Eden's hopes of escaping from the need to make a decision about this latter perilous option were revived, however, later on the same day, 23 October, when Pineau arrived in London and indicated that the Israelis, still at Sèvres, were after all showing signs of willingness to go ahead with an immediate attack on Egypt on the understanding that France and Great Britain would piously seek to separate the combatants. But once again a British representative would have to go to Paris. And now it was definitely spelled out that an early British air attack on Egypt was a *sine qua non* for Israel. Eden, having gone so far as to send Lloyd to meet Ben-Gurion, was now in no mood to baulk and can be presumed to have authorized Pineau to accept the Israeli condition. He also agreed to send a representative to meet the Israelis to clinch matters. For this task he chose Patrick Dean, then a Deputy Under-Secretary at the Foreign Office.

On 24 October Dean, accompanied by Logan, accordingly flew to Paris. They eventually reached an understanding with the French and Israeli representatives given that early British bombing of Egyptian airfields had been pledged. Israel now unequivocally undertook to invade Egypt on 29 October and to threaten the Canal with a major assault. At this point the French produced what they called a 'record' of the discussions. Dean, on Logan's advice, signed it on an *ad referendum* basis. Each of the three parties took away a copy. It was not quite a formal treaty or protocol. All the same, news of its existence dismayed Eden and he later caused the British copy to be destroyed. And he even sent Dean and Logan back to Paris to try to get the French copy destroyed also, something the French refused to do on the grounds that the Israelis would then be left with the only copy. Eden was thus now pitifully anxious to cover his tracks. But the written record was not what mattered. It was surely that Anglo-French–Israeli talks had taken place at all. For far too many people were soon likely to know about this for Eden to have much hope of the conspiracy remaining a secret for long.

Moreover, even if the fact of the Sèvres meeting could have been kept secret, Eden and Lloyd were also surely naive in not realizing how contrived a high-minded Anglo-French intervention on the occasion of the anticipated Israeli invasion would look to the world. First, under the terms of the Sèvres understanding, the Israelis had agreed to move towards the Mitla Pass in order to make it appear that the Canal was threatened. But no expert would have expected them to go in this direction unless collusion was involved. In the absence of collusion, the Israelis' rational objective would surely have been Sharm el-Sheikh to enable them to protect their shipping route to Aquaba. Secondly, again under the terms of the Sèvres understanding, the British were obliged to give the Israelis and Egyptians a mere 12 hours to comply with their ultimatum, far too brief to seem reasonable. But, given the collusion, it made sense: the Israelis needed rapid British action to destroy the Egyptian Air Force which might otherwise attack Israeli cities. In short, the whole operation, even in the best case of the Sèvres meetings remaining secret, was likely to lack plausibility. Even Eden's 'authorized' biographer felt constrained to write: 'It was plainly, as Eden knew, a pretext for achieving the destruction of Nasser. But it was so obvious a pretext that one still wonders why he believed it would not be seen as such.'[24]

It must be presumed, however, that Eden, however foolishly, did expect to deceive many people both at home and abroad. All the same, he was fairly candid with his Cabinet colleagues. True, he obviously did not feel that the terms of the Sèvres understanding could be disclosed in full at the crucial Cabinet held on 25 October (see Appendix II). For one thing the discussion among the three parties had obviously been based on an understanding that what took place would remain secret. And in this respect at least Eden was to prove more a man of honour than his fellow-conspirators. Nevertheless, he left his Cabinet colleagues in no doubt that a showdown was imminent, saying that it now appeared that the Israelis 'were, after all, advancing their military preparations with a view to making an attack on Egypt'. According to Lloyd, he said 'the date might be 29 October'.[25]

For most intelligent people this would surely have seemed to be an acknowledgement that he had maintained the close contacts with the Israelis whose existence, in general terms, had already been communicated to the Cabinet on 23 October. As for actual collusion, he offered this hint:

We must face the risk that we should be accused of collusion with Israel. But this charge was liable to be brought against us in any event; for it could now be assumed that, if an Anglo-French operation were undertaken against Egypt, we should be unable to prevent the Israelis from launching a parallel attack themselves; and it was preferable that we should be seen to be holding the balance between Israel and Egypt rather than appear to be accepting Israeli co-operation in an attack on Egypt alone.[26]

Opinions are always likely to differ about Eden's conduct on 25 October and its implications for modern Cabinet govern-ment. To one writer, Richard Lamb, the Prime Minister was 'specifically untruthful' and engaged in 'arrant dishonesty'.[27] But a less severe judgement is probably in order. At all events, this was no one-man operation and no example of Prime Ministerial rule running riot. All Eden's most senior colleagues knew about the 'collusion'; and Lloyd, not Eden, had of course actually met Ben-Gurion. As for more junior Cabinet Minis-ters, they had been given plenty of hints. And if they did not discover every last detail this may have been at least in part their own fault. For they seem to have been content not to ask penetrating questions about the extent of the contacts with Israel and about the exact degree of foreknowledge possessed by the Prime Minister. And, of course, though several Cabinet Ministers expressed reservations, not one resigned when Eden asked for and received authority to take military action if Israel acted as now expected. Perhaps, then, the Cabinet of 25 October was not as much of an innovation in British consti-tutional practice as some have supposed.

The military phase

On the evening of 29 October the plan, originally sketched by Challe, began to unfold. Israel launched its promised assault on Egypt through the Sinai and posed an immediate threat to the Suez Canal by successfully dropping parachutists in the vicinity of the Mitla Pass.

On the following morning, 30 October, the British Cabinet re-authorized the action which had been initially foreseen and approved in principle at the meeting of 25 October: Egypt and Israel should be required to fall back ten miles on either side of the Canal and consent to an Anglo-French force temporarily occupying the Suez Canal (see Appendix II). Next Mollet and Pineau flew in from Paris to give the appearance of consultation. Then, after lunch, what amounted to ultimatums were presented to the Egyptian and Israeli Ambassadors in London. And, at 4.30 p.m. Eden made an announcement to the House of Commons concerning what had just been done. The Labour Opposition reacted with incredulity and hostility. Any hope that Eden may have had for a muted reaction in that quarter soon vanished: the House formally divided, leaving the government with a majority of only 52.

Even more serious for Eden on 30 October was the reaction of the United States. This was caused in part by two serious misjudgements made in London about how to handle the Americans. First, Lloyd had unwisely granted an interview to Ambassador Aldrich on the morning of 30 October. According to the latter's later account:

I asked Mr Lloyd what the British Government intended to do in view of Israel's action. He replied that he *thought Her Majesty's Government would immediately cite Israel before the Security Council of the United Nations as an aggressor against Egypt*. Believe it or not, that's what he told me that morning they were going to do, but he added that the French Prime Minister and the French Foreign Secretary were on their way to London for consultation and Her Majesty's Government would want to discuss with them before taking action, as they wanted to act in concert with the French. Moreover, he said, the British had shipping and cargo of great value in the Canal and it would be necessary to take this into consideration. In view of all this, Mr Lloyd concluded he could not tell me definitely what action the British would take until after the meeting which was to be held at once with the French, but that he would inform me about their decision immediately after luncheon. I then left Mr Lloyd and reported what he'd said to Washington by cable. At 1.30 p.m. Mr Lloyd's private secretary called Mr James Moffett, my private secretary, and said that Mr Lloyd would have to go directly to the House of Commons after luncheon, so could not see me then. However, Sir Ivone Kirkpatrick . . . would see me at 4.45 and tell me exactly what had been decided.[28]

Perhaps this account should be treated with caution. But it seems clear that Aldrich was deliberately kept in the dark about the intended ultimatum to Egypt and Israel.

Then, to add insult to injury, a message from Eden to Eisenhower setting out what he intended to say in the House of Commons, despatched to Washington only three hours before-hand, failed to reach the President in time to prevent him from first learning of the ultimatums to Egypt and Israel from press reports. This was particularly irksome as Eisenhower was heavily involved in political campaigning, his presidential re-election contest being only a week away. The President retaliated by sending to Eden a stunningly cold and formal message which he went so far as to release to the press:

Dear Mr Prime Minister,

I have just learned from the press of the 12 hour ultimatum which you and the French Government have delivered to the Government of Egypt requiring under threat of forceful intervention the temporary occupation by Anglo-French forces of key positions at Port Said, Ismailia and Suez in the Canal Zone.

I feel I must urgently express to you my deep concern at the prospect of this drastic action even at the very time when the matter is under consideration as it is today by the Security Council. It is my sincere belief that peaceful processes can and should prevail to secure a solution which will restore the armistice conditions as between Israel and Egypt, and also justly settle the controversy with Egypt about the Suez Canal.[29]

Eisenhower and Dulles had also been angered when, on the previous day, the American Ambassador to the United

Nations, Henry Cabot Lodge, had asked his British counter-part, Sir Pierson Dixon, whether the Tripartite Declaration of 1950 did not still bind Great Britain, France and the United States and had been told that it was 'ancient history without current validity'. This led Eisenhower to complain to Dulles that Eden had hitherto failed to make this clear. He added ominously that the American government 'are a government of honour'.[30]

The Americans evidently did not now consider that the British and French governments deserved this accolade. Hence on the evening of 30 October Cabot Lodge felt justified in introducing into the Security Council a resolution de-manding Israeli withdrawal from Egypt and calling on all UN members to refrain from the use or threat of use of force. The British and French forthwith vetoed the American resolution, a step which perhaps followed logically from the Sèvres con-spiracy but one that inevitably astonished the world. The Americans now made common cause with the Soviet Union and on 31 October secured sufficient votes to ensure that the matter was passed on to the General Assembly. That the Americans were thus willing to cooperate with the Soviet Union is, incidentally, a measure of their anger with their allies. For the Soviets at this period were in particularly bad odour as they were in the process of seeking to repress the Hungarian uprising, though they did not enter Budapest until 4 November.

The Egyptians, thus encouraged by American support, naturally rejected the Anglo-French ultimatum. Hence on 31 October the British and the French appeared to be required to begin to honour their obligations to Israel. With their task force already at sea *en route* for Port Said (where it was due to arrive on 6 November), the immediate need was to cripple the Egyptian Air Force. There was, however, an unexpected problem, namely that American civilians were being evacuated from Egypt during the daylight hours of 31 October. This led Eden to postpone plans for the bombing of Egyptian airfields. Israel was thus left vulnerable to Egyptian air strikes for a vital period of 12 hours, contrary to the spirit of the Sèvres under-standing. The Egyptians, however, failed to take advantage of their opportunity and the Anglo-French bombing duly took place on the night of 31 October/1 November. The Israelis could breathe again. But they were thereafter during the Crisis to follow their own narrow interests, showing no particular concern for the fate of Eden.

1 November was marked by further polarization on the British domestic front. For a major confrontation in the Commons took place. Dismayed by the exercise of the British veto at the Security Council and by news of the overnight bombing of Egyptian airfields, Gaitskell now led his party into unequivocal condemnation of the whole enterprise. Scenes of great disorder ensued with the result that the Speaker had to suspend the sitting for half an hour. News of this drama naturally received world-wide coverage and reinforced the resolve of many overseas to speak out in unrestrained language.

Extreme hostility was, in particular, expressed by most Commonwealth leaders, and Pakistan even threatened to resign from the organization. Only Australia and New Zealand could be said to have been in the least degree supportive of the Mother Country. In themselves, the Commonwealth pro- clamations of censure were of only marginal importance. For Eden's Cabinet stood in a long British tradition of making policy without permitting the Dominions, let alone the Colonies, to have any decisive voice. All the same, there were indirect consequences. In particular, Commonwealth hostility undoubtedly encouraged many of Great Britain's critics at the United Nations to become even more bold in their condemna- tions.

Foremost among the critics was of course the United States, as was demonstrated on 2 November at the UN General Assembly. Dulles himself arrived at the rostrum to condemn his allies. The Assembly voted by 65 votes to five in favour of a resolution urging a ceasefire and the withdrawal of British, French and Israeli forces from Egypt. Faced with this un- expectedly rapid and thoroughgoing censure, the British government announced its willingness to see the creation of a UN peacekeeping force to take over the ostensible purpose of their intervention, namely to separate the combatants and protect the Canal. The essentially irresolute Eden was apparently talked into agreeing to this move by Lloyd. It was to contribute greatly to his later difficulties, as will be seen.

On the following day, 3 November, Lester Pearson, the Canadian Foreign Minister, most unhelpfully set about mobilizing support for the rapid creation of a United Nations Emergency Force (UNEF) which the British were now unable to oppose outright. Instead, they were reduced to quibbling about the terms. In particular, they insisted that they and the French must be part of the UNEF and that their forces should land in Egypt as forerunners for the main force.

4 November was to be a traumatic day in London. The Egypt Committee met before and after lunch and the full Cabinet met in the evening. The tidings from Egypt were mixed. The ultimatum and the bombing had *not* led to the fall of Nasser, something which Eden seems to have half-expected. And the Canal had been blocked by deliberately scuttled vessels. But the good news was that Nasser had decided to withdraw many of his troops from the Suez Canal Zone to defend Cairo. This meant that an airborne landing by British and French forces at Port Said and Port Fuad on 5 November had suddenly become a serious possibility, a day before the seaborne landings were scheduled to take place. Getting a foothold on Egyptian soil a day earlier than expected had of course great attractions. For, with UN and American threats growing, every hour was vital if a total abortion of the enterprise was to be avoided.

Eden was eager to proceed with airborne landings, as were the French. But among his colleagues doubts were raised. At the Egypt Committee, for example, Lloyd warned that there was talk in New York of oil sanctions being imposed. Macmillan apparently greeted this news with an unexpected cry of: 'Oil sanctions. That finishes it.'[31] There was also increasing evidence, known to a few, that the American Sixth Fleet had actually been shadowing the Anglo-French task force in a fashion that might be construed as menacing. Matters were made no easier for Eden by the knowledge that Mountbatten had asked to be allowed to resign as First Sea Lord but had consented to continue to serve only on receiving a written military order.

More depressing still was news that both Egypt and Israel

were apparently willing to respond positively to the UN call for a ceasefire. This could be held to render unnecessary the Anglo-French landings, including the new airborne option for 5 November.

In these circumstances Eden decided that the full Cabinet, meeting on the evening of 4 November, must choose among three broad options: to proceed with the invasion of Egypt, while expressing willingness eventually to transfer authority to a UNEF from which the British and the French would not be excluded; to suspend landings for 24 hours to permit the picture at New York to become clearer; or to defer military action indefinitely. Eden favoured the first course. But he faced dramatic opposition from Butler who, when a vote was taken, had the support of at least five colleagues, namely Kilmuir, Salisbury, Monckton, Derek Heathcoat Amory (Minister of Agriculture) and Patrick Buchan-Hepburn (Minister of Works). About 12 colleagues voted for the Prime Minister's approach, including Macmillan notwithstanding his earlier 'wobble'.

Butler's later account of this division and its sequel is controversial:

I took the line that were the news [about a pending Israeli–Egyptian ceasefire] correct, we could not possibly continue our expedition. It had not been my idea to announce that we were going in to stop hostilities, but if they had already stopped we had no justification for invasion. This argument, which was backed by Lord Salisbury, seemed to nonplus the Prime Minister. He said he must go upstairs and consider his position. If he could not have united support, the situation might arise in which someone else might have to take over from him.[32]

This claim that Eden in effect threatened to resign is not confirmed in the Cabinet Minutes, which do not, however, record any adjournment either. The diary of Clarissa Eden (now Countess of Avon) does confirm, on the other hand, that a break did indeed take place. So was the resignation threat also made? The likelihood is that it was, but not in front of the full Cabinet, as Butler implied. According to Eden's 'authorized' biographer:

There was an adjournment as the Government was awaiting further information on the Israeli position ... What actually happened was that Eden took Butler, Macmillan and Salisbury aside and, as Clarissa Eden's diaries describe the conversation, told them that 'if they wouldn't go on then he would have to resign. Rab said if he did resign no one could form a Government.' Macmillan and Salisbury agreed. The adjournment was to await the Israeli response to the conditions of the UN.[33]

Yet another account was published by political journalist James Margach (who did not name his source):

Butler says that the debate 'seemed to nonplus the Prime Minister. He said he must go upstairs and consider his position.' In fact, the scene was much more moving. Eden was emotionally overcome. He broke down in tears and cried: 'You are all deserting me.' He was in total collapse, weeping unashamedly. Then he went upstairs to compose himself. For such is the agony of power when it denies you.[34]

Of these three accounts, Lady Avon's appears to be the more plausible.

Eden's widow's diary is also probably more reliable than any other source about what occurred when the Cabinet meeting resumed. When told that news had been received that the Israelis had not after all agreed to a ceasefire on terms acceptable to the United Nations, 'Everyone laughed and banged the table with relief – except [Nigel] Birch [Air Minister, not a member of the Cabinet] and Monckton who looked glum.'[35] The Cabinet now consented unanimously to airborne landings proceeding on the following day. Not even Monckton appears to have resisted.

On 5 November British and French paratroops landed successfully at the northern end of the Suez Canal. Port Fuad was quickly secured. Port Said, a larger city, did not surrender. But the allied forces established themselves on its outskirts while awaiting the main seaborne task force. This duly arrived on the following day and met with no major armed resistance. But there was a fair amount of sniper fire and this led to robust methods being adopted by the British and French forces. Naval guns were fired at Port Said. And allied forces ashore responded to sniping in a fashion that inevitably involved innocent civilian casualties. On 5 November, too, some bombing of the outskirts of Cairo had taken place. The final deathtoll would seem to have approached 1,000 on the Egyptian side but to have barely reached double figures in the cases of Great Britain and France.

General Hugh Stockwell, the Supreme Commander of the allied task force, later claimed that the whole length of the Canal would have been captured within 48 hours of the main seaborne landings. But within hours of these landings he was being told to expect an order for a premature ceasefire. Later in the day this became definite and was fixed for midnight (London time). The task force had by that stage seized about one-third of the Canal.

The ceasefire

What had led to this astonishing anticlimax which was to cause dismay to British and French troops and was to be hailed by Nasser as a victory? No exact explanation may ever be known. But it would seem that Eden and Macmillan, for differing reasons, both became convinced, either just before or during the Cabinet meeting held on the morning of 6 November, that the enterprise would have to be halted. For Macmillan, according to his own account, the decisive consideration was the plight of sterling. A run, long expected by the Treasury, had developed and the Chancellor's line, whether sincere or not, was that an immediate standby support from the International Monetary Fund was essential. The procedure involved, normally routine, could in practice be blocked by the Americans. 'It was only while the Cabinet was in session', wrote Macmillan in his memoirs, 'that I received the reply that the American Government would not agree to the technical procedure until we had agreed to the ceasefire.'[36] The Cabinet Minutes, which are unusually brief and uninformative, do not confirm that the Chancellor made use of this information to influence his colleagues in favour of a ceasefire but it seems safe to assume that he did so.

It is, incidentally, worth noting that Macmillan had long been aware that a run on the pound was a serious possibility if the country resorted to force against Egypt (and perhaps even if it did not). Sir Edward Bridges, the Permanent Secretary to the Treasury, wrote to Macmillan on 7 September:

Very broadly it seems to us that unless we can secure at least United States support and a fairly unified Commonwealth, then it is not possible to predict either the exact timing or the magnitude of the strains which are likely to come upon our currency. At the worst, however, the strains might be so great that, whatever precautionary measures were taken, we should be unable to maintain the value of the currency.

Macmillan minuted his agreement: 'What this points to . . . is the vital necessity from the point of view of our currency and our economy of ensuring that we do not go it alone, and that we have the maximum United States support.'[37] Yet not only did Macmillan continue to be an unrestrained 'hawk', he also made no effective plans to deal with the crisis that he and Bridges anticipated. Moreover, it is not clear that he made Eden, let alone the full Cabinet, aware of the magnitude of the potential sterling problem, at least until all concerned were too deeply committed to withdraw without a grievous loss of face.

For Eden the Cabinet of 6 November was probably also seen as an unavoidable turning point but for other reasons. He may have found Macmillan's conduct unforgiveable; he referred in his memoirs to the fact that 'there are weak sisters in any crisis and sometimes they will be found among those who were toughest at the outset of the journey.'[38] But he probably had already made up his mind to favour an immediate ceasefire before the Cabinet met. And financial problems, which he only ever dimly understood, may not have mattered most. Four other points were probably of at least equal importance, though which, if any, was decisive is impossible to say. First, he may have been influenced by sulphurous communications from Eisenhower, now in sole charge of American foreign policy with Dulles in hospital from 3 November for a cancer operation. Secondly, he may have been worried by prospects that the Soviets could intervene in some fashion following the receipt on 5 November of a telegram from Premier Nikolai Bulganin threatening rocket attacks. Thirdly, he may have been influenced by unusually vigorous messages from Dixon spelling out just how damaging the operation was proving to Great Britain's reputation at the United Nations. Finally, he had received an unwelcome message from Dag Hammarskjöld, the UN Secretary-General, to the effect that Israel had after all agreed to a ceasefire on terms that seemed acceptable.

The Cabinet Minutes for 6 November do not attribute any particular opinions to the Prime Minister (see Appendix II). But Lloyd's line is recorded and may be presumed to have been close to that which Eden wished to see presented. The Foreign Secretary had three points. First, he stressed the urgency of regaining the initiative in New York where there was still 'an opportunity to carry with us the more moderate sections of opinion in the General Assembly'. Secondly, he wanted to enlist the maximum sympathy and support from the Americans. Finally, he urged that: 'We must not appear to be yielding in face of Soviet threats.'[39]

The implications of the last point, however, suggested to some unnamed Cabinet colleagues that an immediate ceasefire was desirable, and perhaps that is what Lloyd intended. For otherwise the British might be driven to accept such a ceasefire *after* Soviet actions had followed the threats. The fear was not apparently that the Soviets would make rocket attacks on British cities but that they would intervene in the Middle East itself. According to the Cabinet Minutes:

It would still be practicable to proceed with the Anglo-French occupation of the Canal Area, regardless of opposition from any quarter. But, if we adopted this course, we must reckon with the possibility of a Soviet invasion of Syria or some other area in the Middle East, and possibly a direct Soviet attack on the Anglo-French forces in the Canal area.[40]

The Chiefs of Staff appear to have been among those impressed by this logic. At all events, in the aftermath of the ceasefire, they stated in a memorandum that one reason for the government decision of 6 November was 'the possibility of Russian intervention and the consequent necessity for realigning ourselves alongside the United States from whom our previous actions have estranged us'.[41]

Eden probably shared these apprehensions about possible Soviet moves on the conventional military level. But they may have been decisively reinforced by recollections of the lack of support he had received from six colleagues two days earlier when they had discussed the then false assumption that the Israelis had agreed to a ceasefire. Now that it once again appeared to be valid, he may not have relished going over the same ground again in a deteriorating situation.

For indications that Eden may also have been influenced by Eisenhower's angry outbursts, we have French testimony. Later, on 6 November, when the British Cabinet had taken their decision, these were said by Pineau to have been the main grounds, together with the threats to sterling, adduced by Eden in explaining his *volte face* to Mollet.[42]

As for Dixon's role, we have his own claim, in his memoirs, that he spoke on the telephone to Eden at 8.30 a.m. just before the Cabinet met.[43] What has also now come to light is the text of a telegram Dixon sent to Eden on the evening of 5 November. It includes the following remarkably candid passages occasioned by news of the further bombing of Cairo:

6. You will recall that two days ago (my telegram No.1033) I felt constrained to warn you that if there was any bombing of open cities with resulting loss of civilian life it would make our proposals seem completely cynical and entirely undermine our position here. Again in my telegram No.1035 I urged that, unless we could announce that Anglo-French forces were suspending all further military activities until we knew that the United Nations were prepared to deal with the whole situation effectively, there would be no chance of our being able to move towards our objectives without alienating the whole world.

7. I must again repeat this warning with renewed emphasis.

8. For the purposes of today's proceedings it would be useful if I could have:

    (a) A governmental statement on our bombing policy;

    (b) Up-to-date figures, if available, of Egyptian casualties so far caused in our operations, in particular of civilian personnel;

    (c) Information as to when our limited operation with its limited objectives is going to stop.

9. You will realize that monstrously unjust as it may be in the light of

the precautions which General Keightley is taking (and which I realize places him in a grave dilemma in view of his responsibility for British military personnel and for the success of the operation entrusted to him) we are inevitably being placed in the same low category as the Russians in their bombing of Budapest. I do not see how we can carry much conviction in our protests against the Russian bombing of Budapest if we are ourselves bombing Cairo.[44]

Whichever factor was most decisive may, in short, never be known. But at all events, Eden and all his senior colleagues finally accepted on the morning of the 6 November that there must be a ceasefire that day. It remained for Eden to inform Mollet and await the reluctant acquiescence of the French Cabinet which was soon forthcoming. At 6 p.m. Eden duly rose in the House of Commons to make the humiliating public announcement that a ceasefire would come into force at midnight (London time).

Notes

1 Quoted in David Carlton, *Anthony Eden: a Biography* (London, 1981), p. 430.
2 Anthony Nutting, *No End of a Lesson: the Story of Suez* (London, 1967), p. 94.
3 Leon D. Epstein, *British Politics in the Suez Crisis* (London, 1964), pp. 46–7.
4 Nutting, *No End of a Lesson*, p. 83.
5 See Robert Rhodes James, *Anthony Eden* (London, 1986), p. 527.
6 Anthony Eden, *Full Circle* (London, 1960), p. 508.
7 Richard Lamb, *The Failure of the Eden Government* (London, 1987), pp. 231–2.
8 Jebb to Lloyd, 17 October 1956 quoted in Lamb, *The Failure of the Eden Government*, pp. 233–4.
9 Selwyn Lloyd, *Suez 1956: a Personal Account* (London, 1978), p. 175.
10 Moshe Dayan, *Story of my Life* (London, 1976), p. 174.
11 Lloyd, *Suez 1956*, p. 175. See also Lloyd's contemporary account in FO 800/728, PRO.
12 Quoted in Lamb, *The Failure of the Eden Government*, p. 242.
13 Cab. 128/30, PRO.

14 Quoted in Lamb, *The Failure of the Eden Government*, p. 236.

15 Lord Butler, *The Art of the Possible* (London, 1971), p. 192.

16 Lloyd, *Suez 1956*, p. 180.

17 Rhodes James, *Anthony Eden*, p. 532.

18 Lamb, *The Failure of the Eden Government*, p. vii.

19 For further details see John Zametica, 'Suez: the secret plan', *The Spectator*, 17 January 1987.

20 Donald Logan, 'Collusion at Suez', *The Financial Times*, 8 November 1986; and Pineau quoted in Carlton, *Anthony Eden*, pp. 436–7.

21 Logan, 'Collusion at Suez'.

22 Cab. 128/30 (Confidential Annex), PRO.

23 Cab. 128/30, PRO.

24 Rhodes James, *Anthony Eden*, p. 533.

25 Cab. 128/30, PRO; Lloyd, *Suez 1956*, p. 188.

26 Cab. 128/30, PRO.

27 Lamb, *The Failure of the Eden Government*, p. 243.

28 Aldrich Recollections quoted in Carlton, *Anthony Eden*, p. 444.

29 Eisenhower to Eden, 30 October 1956, Prem. 11/1105, PRO.

30 Record of telephone conversation between Eisenhower and Dulles, 30 October 1956, Eisenhower Papers, quoted in Carlton, *Anthony Eden*, pp. 444–5.

31 Lloyd, *Suez 1956*, p. 206. See also Rhodes James, *Anthony Eden*, p. 565n. Macmillan's interjection is not confirmed in the Minutes of the Egypt Committee, Cab. 134/1216.

32 Butler, *The Art of the Possible*, p. 193.

33 Cab. 128/30, PRO; and Rhodes James, *Anthony Eden*, p. 567.

34 James Margach, *The Abuse of Power* (London, 1978), p. 113.

35 Rhodes James, *Anthony Eden*, p. 567.

36 Harold Macmillan, *Riding the Storm, 1956–1959* (London, 1971), p. 164.

37 Quoted in Peter Hennessy, 'The scars of Suez', *The Listener*, 5 February 1987.

38 Eden, *Full Circle*, p. 557.

39 Cab. 128/30, PRO.

40 Ibid.

41 Memorandum by the Chiefs of Staff for the Egypt Committee, 8 November 1956, Cab. 134/1217. See Appendix III.

42 Christian Pineau, *1956. Suez* (Paris, 1976), pp. 175–6.

43 Piers Dixon, *Double Diploma: the Life of Sir Pierson Dixon, Don and Diplomat* (London, 1968), pp. 271–2.

44 Prem. 11/1105, PRO.

5 The Aftermath

The Anglo–American rift

With the announcement of a ceasefire the humiliation of Great Britain had in fact only just begun, although Eden and some of his colleagues seem at first to have hoped that the damage could be limited. But, as with Germany after the Armistice of 11 November 1918, the country's position grew steadily weaker. As a result the terms of settlement finally inflicted were considerably more severe than would at first have seemed likely to be accepted by any government that had not actually been brought by outright military defeat to the point of unconditional surrender. In short, the distinction between a reluctantly conceded armistice and unconditional surrender can in practice be illusory. For once military action has been halted, it may not be practical politics to contemplate any resumption.

That Great Britain might be on just such a slippery slope to total humiliation was borne in upon Eden within 24 hours of the announcement of the ceasefire. For in three telephone conversations with Eisenhower on 7 November he was forced to recognize that the United States simply might not be interested in pursuing policies that would have had the effect of partially saving his country's (and his own) face. In the first conversation Eden congratulated Eisenhower on his re-election as President – the results having just been announced – and went on to propose that he and Mollet visit Washington forthwith. The President, no doubt in a state of some euphoria at his personal victory, indicated conditional approval of the plan and spoke of recent events as being like 'a family spat'.[1] This raised Eden's hopes that the three Western powers might now be able to harmonize their policies with respect to the Middle East and collectively use the bargaining power (or 'gage' as Eden and Lloyd called it) of the Anglo-French presence in Egypt to force concessions from Nasser on a variety of issues including the future of the Canal. But, after speaking to various aides, the President telephoned again to seek clarification about the purpose of the meeting. He was willing to discuss NATO matters and the Soviet threat but so far as the Middle East was concerned he was anxious to know that the British and the French would not seek to avoid early withdrawal from Egypt and would support the despatch of a United Nations Emergency Force (UNEF) from which all the great powers would be excluded. He certainly did not wish the meeting to result in a divided communiqué. In his desperation to secure a reconciliation with the Americans, Eden attempted to offer full reassurance to Eisenhower; and he had indeed already intimated to his doubtful Cabinet colleagues that in his view the British and French should not insist on participating in any UNEF (which was on the point of approval at the United Nations in New York). Eisenhower appeared to be satisfied and agreed to a public announcement of the visit being made at 4 p.m. London time. But less than half an hour before this was due to happen he put through a third telephone call to Eden and brusquely indicated that after further consultations with his advisers (incidentally including Dulles who was still in hospital for the cancer operation of 3 November) he had concluded that the visit must be 'postponed'.[2] He brushed aside Eden's protests and thereafter would have almost nothing more to do with him. Eisenhower's refusal is said to have been deeply painful to Eden. An official with him at the time saw 'his face harden and then sag'. The official added that 'what remained of his spirit seemed to have gone'.[3]

Lacking the diversionary advantage of a visit to Washington, Eden now had to face the House of Commons for a vote of confidence. This took place on 8 November. The government survived but there was no disguising the unease in the Conservative ranks. Eight Conservatives, all opponents of the Anglo-French intervention, abstained. But the Conservative critics of the ceasefire, who were of course much more numerous, stayed loyal in the lobbies, for they could scarcely risk bringing down the government if the only likely consequence would be to put Labour into office.

On 11 November Eden made one last despairing attempt to persuade Eisenhower to come to his rescue. Mollet had seen fit to send what amounted to a begging letter to the President asking him to alter his earlier decision and permit an early Anglo-French visit to Washington. Eden endorsed his plea. The President, perhaps realizing for the first time the extent to which he was master of the situation, returned an uncompromising rebuff. He now explicitly made the withdrawal of the Anglo-French forces and their replacement by a UNEF an absolute precondition: after it had been carried out successfully, 'we should then be able to consider arrangements for a meeting.'[4] He then embarked on a course that amounted to nothing less than one of threatening economic sanctions against his allies unless they rapidly bowed the knee in the Middle East. Both allies were dependent on American oil supplies during whatever period the Canal would remain blocked, petrol rationing having to be introduced in Great Britain on 17 December. The British government, in addition, still stood in urgent need of loans to bolster sterling. With brutal frankness, American officials spelled out to their British and French counterparts that all assistance was dependent on unconditional compliance with UN demands with respect to the Middle East. No face-saving formulas were to be offered either by the United States or by Dag Hammarskjöld, the UN Secretary-General. The composition of the UNEF was not open for negotiation. Nor was the future regime for controlling the Canal. And proffered British and French assistance in clearing the entire Canal was rejected out of hand at the exultant Nasser's insistence. In short, a public announcement of unconditional Anglo-French withdrawal from Egypt by a specified date was demanded. This punitive approach was to be relentlessly pursued in the ensuing weeks.

Desperate to salvage something from the wreck, Lloyd arrived in New York on 13 November ostensibly to have discussions at the United Nations. In practice, he sought to open negotiations with the Americans and with Eisenhower in particular. But the President flatly refused to meet him. By now Eisenhower and his entourage had had time to reflect on the extent to which they had been deliberately deceived by their allies and had also received details from French sources of the extent of the Sèvres conspiracy. And their collective anger against Eden and Lloyd in particular seems as a result to have greatly intensified. They became imbued with remarkable self-righteousness, and they convinced themselves that any compromise would be a betrayal of principle and would cost them all chance of having future good standing in the Middle East.

In his memoirs, Eden reflected bitterly on this turn of events. Referring to his decision to agree to a ceasefire, he wrote:

We would have taken a second, and maybe a third, look at the problem had we understood what was to come. We were ashore with a sufficient force to hold Port Said. We held a gage ... Out of this situation intelligent international statesmanship should, we thought, be able to shape a lasting settlement for the Arab–Israeli conflict and for the future of the canal. We had not understood that, so far from doing this, the United Nations, and in particular the United States, would insist that all the advantages gained must be thrown away before serious negotiation began. This was the most calamitous of all errors. Had we expected it to be perpetrated, our course might have been otherwise, but we could not know. As it seems to me, the major mistakes were made, not before the ceasefire or in that decision, but after it. I did not foresee them.[5]

But, as has been seen, it is doubtful whether the British Cabinet in reality had had any practical alternative other than to agree to a ceasefire as matters stood on 6 November. And now in the matter of withdrawing from Egypt the same Cabinet had really no choice at all other than to yield to overwhelming American pressure. The only question was whether to accept the inevitable at once or whether to prolong the agony.

Two crucial meetings on 15 and 16 November – the first of the Egypt Committee, the second of the full Cabinet – saw the beginnings of the debate on the grim alternatives.[6] The harsh nature of the American terms for financial assistance was in fact by now already known to Ministers. Yet Eden attempted to rally the 'hawks' by somewhat capriciously insisting that withdrawal from Egypt could not be unconditional. He told the Egypt Committee:

we could not allow ourselves to be put into the insecure position of having to withdraw our troops with no adequate satisfaction regarding the re-opening of the Canal.

. . . we would be prepared to remove our troops, unit by unit, in a phased operation as the United Nations forces came in. We could not, however, accept a condition that our forces should have been totally withdrawn before any agreement for clearing the Canal could become operative.

This, on Eden's part, however, was simply failing to come to terms with the magnitude of the problem: a return to the indecisiveness that had marked his conduct of the Suez Crisis before mid-October. If capitulation was to be avoided there was only one theoretical way out: a serious alternative strategy would have to be adopted and this would inevitably have involved not only terminating the ceasefire and seizing the entire Canal, as the Chiefs of Staff spelled out, but would also have meant accepting a sterling devaluation and an outright confrontation with the United States and perhaps also the Soviet Union. But, as Eden presumably realized, no such major strategic rethink was in the realm of practical politics. He was thus once again completely without options and reduced to waiting, as in the early days of October, for something to turn up. This time, however, Challe and Gazier did not put in an appearance.

Fate's next blow for Eden came on 18 November when he felt compelled to consult Sir Horace Evans and other doctors about his state of health. They advised a period of rest, preferably in a sunny climate. He all too readily agreed and went on to accept an offer from Ann and Ian Fleming (of 'James Bond' fame) to make use of their home in a remote corner of Jamaica. A public announcement was made on 21 November and he and his wife flew out of London on 23 November with the issue of withdrawal still essentially unresolved. In the *Manchester Guardian* the journalist Randolph Churchill, son of Sir Winston, compared Eden's attitude with Hitler's refusal to quit Stalingrad, adding 'But even Hitler did not winter in Jamaica.'[7]

The capitulation

Butler was left in nominal charge. It was, however, to be Macmillan who was to take the greatest advantage of Eden's absence. On the evening of 18 November, on hearing of the doctors' advice to Eden, he moved with indecent alacrity to ingratiate himself with Eisenhower. He sought out Ambassador Aldrich and appears to have indicated that Eden would not be returning from Jamaica as Prime Minister. He himself asked to be allowed to visit Eisenhower as soon as possible. No invitation resulted. But the President did encourage Aldrich to enter into backstairs discussions during the ensuing days not only with Macmillan but with Butler and Salisbury as well. The basic subject matter was of course the provision of American assistance in return for unconditional withdrawal from Egypt. But the future of Eden was also candidly raised. And neither the Prime Minister himself nor the Foreign Office was informed that these talks were taking place.

Aldrich did not relish the role he was being asked to play by the White House and he was, moreover, severely critical of Eisenhower's entire handling of the situation after the cease-fire. As he subsequently recalled:

I myself was surprised at the vitriolic nature of Eisenhower's reaction to what happened. I think it was unstatesmanlike; indeed I think it was a dreadful thing, the way the United States Government permitted itself to act towards Eden because of pique or petulance ... the President just went off the deep end. He wouldn't have anything further to do with Eden at all. He wouldn't even communicate with him ... The problem was solved in a manner which never has been made public even now, although perhaps some people suspected it at the time ... Salisbury and Rab Butler and Harold Macmillan were willing to discuss with me the situation which had arisen between the United States and Great Britain and I became the channel of communication between them and Washington ... And for the period of time between the attack on Egypt to the time Eden retired and

Macmillan became Prime Minister I would say that all important diplomatic exchanges in London between the United States and Great Britain took place between myself and those three members of the Cabinet. The meetings were confidential because it became necessary to bypass the Prime Minister and the Foreign Secretary. After a few days of this procedure I decided I had to get direct authority from Washington to continue what I was doing, because I was having conferences with those three men that were entirely off the record and I had to assume that if they thought it necessary they would talk to Eden. Eden soon reached the point where he was incapable of assuming responsibility and it was perfectly obvious that he'd have to be superseded.[8]

Aldrich was in error in implying that all the exchanges went through him. For Butler established an independent channel by telephone to George Humphrey, the US Treasury Secretary, who was in close touch with Eisenhower. Nevertheless, the collusion to which Aldrich referred was certainly taking place as is confirmed by the following record of a telephone conversation held on 20 November between the Ambassador and the President himself:

President: We have been getting your messages, and I want to make an inquiry. You are dealing with at least one person – maybe two or three – on a very personal basis. Is it possible for you, without embarrassment, to get together the two you mentioned in one of your messages?

Aldrich: Yes, one of them I have just been playing bridge with. Perhaps I can stop him.

President: I'd rather you talk to both together. You know who I mean? One has the same name as my predecessor at Columbia University Presidency [Butler]; the other was with me in the war [Macmillan].

Aldrich: I know the one with you in the war. Oh yes, now I've got it.

President: Could you get them informally and say of course we are interested and sympathetic, and as soon as things happen that we anticipate, we can furnish 'a lot of fig leaves'.

Aldrich: I certainly can say that.

President: Will that be enough to get the boys moving?

Aldrich: I think it will be.

President: Herb [Hoover, Under-Secretary at the State Department] probably will send you a cable later tonight. You see, we don't want to be in a position of interfering between those two [Butler and Macmillan]. But we want to have you personally tell them. They are both good friends.[9]

The 'fig leaves' presumably consisted of American financial assistance. As for the 'things' happening 'that we anticipate', Eisenhower undoubtedly had in view an announcement of a date for unconditional withdrawal from Egypt. But he may also have been hoping for confirmation that Eden would indeed be retiring. That he had been led to expect this seems clear. As one well-placed American source has written 'it was my definite understanding that when Eden took his first trip to Jamaica, there was no intention that he would return as Prime Minister. It was explained that this was an example of tactful British finesse.'[10]

Macmillan and Butler may both be presumed to have had at very least high expectations that Eden would quit. Hence their conduct during the latter's absence in Jamaica can hardly have been unaffected by a desire on both their parts not to lose the confidence of their Cabinet colleagues in circumstances where one or other was probably on the point of being invited by the Queen to become Prime Minister. At all events, both men during the last days of November seem to have decided that they must distance themselves from Eden's line of refusing unconditional surrender. Of the two, however, Macmillan proved to be the more bold in forcing the Cabinet to face the harsh facts of the situation. And, paradoxically, this decisiveness may have created an ultimately favourable impression on the colleagues when a choice for Prime Minister had to be made. As Chancellor of the Exchequer he was able, in particular, to stress the importance of making a clear and early decision so that American financial assistance might be in place ahead of the announcement of the monthly level of foreign reserves due to be made on 3 or, at the latest, 4 December. He had support from the Treasury and the Bank of England in arguing that the figures were likely to be so catastrophic that devaluation would otherwise be unavoidable. 'Economic sanctions' for once were working!

The denouement came in successive Cabinet meetings held

on the last four days of November. Gradually, Macmillan increased the pressure on his despairing colleagues. And all the news from across the Atlantic reinforced his resolve to put an end to further indecision. Indicative of what was to come was the passing in the UN General Assembly on 24 November of an Afro-Asian-sponsored motion of censure on Great Britain, France and Israel by 63 votes to five. An attempt to carry a softening amendment, sponsored by Belgium, failed as a direct result of an American decision to abstain. Important, too, was a telegram from Sir Harold Caccia, the newly appointed British Ambassador in Washington. He reported that at a meeting on 28 November Humphrey had revealed no willingness to grant immediate financial assistance to Great Britain. The US Treasury Secretary, according to Caccia, even went so far as to state that:

in the eyes of the world Egypt had been invaded by us and as long as she remained occupied, she would have world sympathy and United States support. If the United Kingdom, by remaining in Port Said, appeared to exert force over negotiations for the clearing of the Canal or the settlement of the future regime for the Canal, the world would never believe that these negotiations were not held at gun-point. Humphrey more than once used the simile that the United Kingdom was an armed burglar who had climbed in through the window while Nasser was the house-holder in his nightshirt appealing to the world for protection.[11]

Such robust language could scarcely leave any doubts in London as to the extent of American resolve. This message was further reinforced by Lloyd who returned from New York to address his Cabinet colleagues on 28 November. According to his own account, he felt that his failure in the United States had made it appropriate that he should tender his resignation.[12] His colleagues dissuaded him from taking so damaging a step. But they could not fail to see that further bargaining with the United States was quite unlikely to yield any dividends.

On 30 November the Cabinet accordingly decided in principle to capitulate. Lloyd was appointed to make a formal announcement in the House of Commons on 3 December. Meanwhile, Caccia was instructed to inform the Americans.

He obtained an appointment with Murphy of the US State Department and indicated that the British agreed to unconditional withdrawal from Egypt. But even this was not enough. Caccia reported to London:

After I had gone carefully over the points made in your telegram, I asked whether this would be sufficient pledge on our behalf to enable action on the United States side to follow. Mr Murphy said that unfortunately it would not satisfy the United States Government so far as action over sterling was concerned. What was needed was a definite date.

I said that I must ask Mr Murphy to ensure that this was reconsidered at the highest level. An Englishman's word was his bond. If the United States Government were now going to act as if they doubted our word, he must know that the results would be most damaging. He knew us. The President knew us, and had more than once expressed his determination to strengthen the alliance. To say the least the present decision of the United States Government would gravely set back that purpose.

Mr Murphy said that there was no question of the United States Government doubting the word of Her Majesty's Government. What they had in mind was the effect on other people in the Middle Eastern area of our failure to give even a target date.[13]

One historian has commented: 'It almost passes belief that a supposedly pro-British senior American diplomat could have spoken in such terms to the British Ambassador.'[14] But this is to leave out of account the British government's continuing mendacity with respect to the collusion with France and Israel and, in particular, the deliberate misleading of Aldrich on 30 October. In short, what could be seen to be more incredible is that in these circumstances Caccia should have been so insensitive as to prate on about an Englishman's word being his bond. But perhaps the explanation was that Caccia himself was at this time largely in the dark about the extent to which his country had recently engaged in a dishonourable conspiracy.

Understandable American doubts were finally resolved, however, when on 3 December Lloyd announced in the House of Commons not only unconditional withdrawal in principle but also stated that a timetable would be agreed between Keightley and the UNEF Commander. This turned out to involve the last British and French troops departing by 22 December. In these circumstances American financial support was provided and sterling was 'saved'.

Lloyd's announcement of what amounted to British surrender of 3 December was, in the words of Eden's 'authorized' biographer, 'a terrible occasion'.[15] The reaction of his subject, still in Jamaica, may be imagined. He had been kept informed in a somewhat cursory fashion about the course of events and had in turn sent messages to London indicating his unease at the slide to capitulation. But in the final analysis he characteristically acquiesced in what was done. To be sure, in later years he blamed Macmillan for too rapidly yielding to American pressure. Yet it is difficult to see how had he been personally in charge he could have avoided a similar surrender in the face of the deadline for sterling that 3 December represented. Indeed, in some moods he seems to have grasped how hopeless the situation had become. For example, on a visit to his old chief in 1958 Lloyd brought up the topic of his own threat of resignation made on 28 November, offering the not very persuasive view that 'we would all have been in a much stronger position if I had been allowed to carry out my intention to resign'; Eden, according to Lloyd, replied that 'that was the moment when we all should have resigned.'[16]

Eden: the final days

Given the magnitude of the humiliation endured by his government on 3 December it seems remarkable that Eden should have returned to London on 14 December in apparent high spirits and that he seemingly supposed that now he no longer felt ill he would be able to resume his premiership without undue difficulty. If this was indeed his expectation he was soon to be crushingly disillusioned. Visits to the House of Commons on 17, 18 and 20 December were of crucial importance. On the first occasion he entered the Chamber but was received by Conservative MPs with an embarrassing lack of cheers. On the second occasion he addressed the 1922 Committee of Conservative backbenchers and, according to an admittedly hostile witness, he was simply unable to handle a question about the status of the Tripartite Declaration, stating that he had not got the point in his head.[17] Finally, on 20 December he was drawn into making statements in the Chamber about alleged 'collusion'. Under severe pressure he twice lied blatantly, stating that 'there were no plans to get together to attack Egypt' and that 'there was not foreknowledge that Israel would attack Egypt'.[18]

Eden and his wife spent Christmas at Chequers and no doubt reviewed their position. To Kilmuir, one of his guests, he expressed doubts about the possibility of carrying on.[19] His health was no doubt a factor. But he cannot have failed to understand by now that his authority over his own Party had been decisively undermined by the capitulation of 3 December. He may have hoped while in Jamaica that blame would fall on the colleagues he had left in charge and that he would be able to return with much the same standing as he had possessed on his departure from London on 23 November. By Christmas he knew otherwise. He faced another problem that was also essentially insoluble: too many people in at least four countries knew enough about the Sèvres meetings to make it inconceivable that he could for long avoid exposure as one who had lied to Parliament.

Meanwhile, what of Eden's not particularly loyal lieutenants? The picture is still rather murky. But we do know that Salisbury visited the Queen at Sandringham at the turn of the year.[20] And we have reason to believe, on the basis of what Mountbatten later made known, that the Queen (Mountbatten's niece) had been personally opposed to the Suez Operation.[21] We also know that the Queen, Butler and Eden all shared the same doctor, namely Evans. Was it, then, entirely coincidental that the latter should soon after have advised the Prime Minister to retire on health grounds? All that can be said with certainty is that Eden accepted the advice and visited Sandringham on 8 January 1957 to inform the Queen. On the following day he formally resigned in a ceremony at Buckingham Palace. He also made known his intention to resign his Commons seat.

Several private letters may throw a little light on how and why Eden's departure came when it did. First, on 14 January,

Evans wrote to Butler (who needless to say had no knowledge of medicine) expressing gratitude for 'your help and guidance over my difficult problem with AE [Eden]'. He added: 'Here we have made, I have no doubt, the right decision.'[22] Secondly, the following correspondence took place between the usually well-informed Brendan Bracken, who was close to Churchill, and the press baron Lord Beaverbrook:

23 January 1957: Bracken to Beaverbrook
The main reason for Eden's departure is not the one circulated by politicians and the press. The reason is political, but as it involves a secret stuffed with dynamite I can't put it in a letter. This seems melodramatic but, alas, it is only too true and you will agree when you hear it. If Eden had been of tougher fibre he could, I am sure, have brazened it out.

29 January 1957: Beaverbrook to Bracken
I can guess from your mention of political secrets, stuffed with dynamite, just what occurred. Political assassination has become a habit in Great Britain, for, of course, Churchill himself was a victim.

4 February 1957: Bracken to Beaverbrook
The 'dynamite' I mentioned in my last letter is collusion, not assassination by colleagues. They were willing, of course, to stab. But our friend brought himself down and needless remorse unnerved him. Secret this![23]

Whether ill health or political pressures were the more decisive in bringing Eden's premiership to an end is thus a point on which speculation is likely to continue.

On 10 January the Queen summoned Macmillan to take over. This was based on advice by the ubiquitous Salisbury, who on the previous day had taken soundings among the members of the Cabinet. (Backbench Conservatives and even Junior Ministers were largely ignored.)

The way was now open for the Suez Crisis finally to be defused. On 16 March 1957 the Israelis reluctantly withdrew, under relentless American pressure, from all areas of Egypt that they had seized in the previous autumn. On 20 and 21 March Macmillan and Lloyd met Eisenhower and Dulles in Bermuda and rapidly re-established good relations. Finally, on 24 April the Suez Canal re-opened and a triumphant Nasser graciously granted to the British and the French the right to use it on the basis of the 'six principles' on offer to them in the previous October. No more has been heard from London from that day to this about the unacceptability of his nationalization 'coup'. It had indeed been no end of a lesson.

Notes

1 Donald Neff, *Warriors at Suez: Eisenhower Takes America into the Middle East* (New York, 1981), p. 414.
2 For details of the discussions in Washington see W. Scott Lucas, 'Suez, the Americans, and the overthrow of Anthony Eden', *LSE Quarterly*, vol. 1, no. 3 (autumn 1987), pp. 230–1.
3 Quoted in Robert Rhodes James, *Anthony Eden* (London, 1986), p. 557.
4 Eisenhower to Eden, 11 November 1956, Prem. 11/1177, PRO.
5 Anthony Eden, *Full Circle* (London, 1960), p. 558.
6 Cab. 134/1216 and Cab. 128/30, PRO.
7 Quoted in Rhodes James, *Anthony Eden*, p. 583.
8 Aldrich recollections quoted in David Carlton, *Anthony Eden: a Biography* (London, 1981), p. 456.
9 Record of telephone conversation between Aldrich and Eisenhower, 20 November 1956, Eisenhower Papers quoted in Carlton, *Anthony Eden*, p.460.
10 Personal communication, 7 June 1979, quoted in Carlton, *Anthony Eden*, p. 462.
11 Quoted in Richard Lamb, *The Failure of the Eden Government* (London, 1987), p. 289.
12 Selwyn Lloyd, *Suez 1956: a Personal Account* (London, 1978), p. 232.
13 Quoted in Lamb, *The Failure of the Eden Government*, pp. 294–5.
14 Ibid., p. 295.
15 Rhodes James, *Anthony Eden*, p. 585.
16 FO 800/728, PRO.
17 For details see Hugh Thomas, *The Suez Affair* (London, 1967), pp. 212–14.
18 For details see Thomas, *The Suez Affair*, pp. 208–12.
19 Lord Kilmuir, *Political Adventure* (London, 1964), pp. 283–4.
20 John Colville, *The Fringes of Power: Downing Street Diaries 1939–1955* (London, 1985), p. 721.

21 Philip Ziegler, *Mountbatten: the Official Biography* (London, 1985), p. 546.

22 Anthony Howard, *RAB: The Life of R. A. Butler* (London, 1987), p. 245.

23 Quoted in Carlton, *Anthony Eden*, p. 465.

6 The Long-term Consequences

Suez and British decline

While the Suez Affair was undoubtedly 'no end of a lesson' for a major section of an entire generation in Great Britain, it does not follow that the country today would be significantly different if the episode had never occurred. Indeed, the present writer once argued that 'with perspective Suez may come to seem a relatively unimportant event in and of itself, more an effect than a cause of national decline.'[1] For the fact is that Great Britain, given its modest base in terms of population and economic strength, had been desperately over-committed throughout the world since at least the end of the Second World War (and maybe for much longer). Retreat from formal and informal Empire was inevitable, as was decline as a global power. This could have been arranged smoothly or otherwise. But reduction to the level of a post-imperial medium power by the 1980s was surely unavoidable. Suez, on this view, was a rather dramatic hiccup in a generally well-managed transition.

The same kind of argument has been applied by Henry Kissinger to the place of the trauma of Vietnam in the somewhat less drastic adjustment to changing circumstances recently made by the United States:

The disintegration of the national consensus on foreign policy is often ascribed to the Vietnam War and Watergate. These events were surely traumatic. But I doubt that they were seminal. The key event was the collapse in the late 1960s of the premises on which American post-war foreign policy had been based. That process may have been speeded and exacerbated by Vietnam, but it would surely have happened without it.

When America ended its isolation after the second world war, an atomic monopoly gave it a margin of security unprecedented in history. As late as 1950 the United States produced 52% of all the world's goods and services. America, by itself, represented the global balance of power. American alliances were, in effect, unilateral guarantees. Recognised problems could be overwhelmed with resources.

By the late 1960s these conditions were disappearing. Nuclear parity was upon us. As Western Europe and Japan recovered and other nations industrialised, America's percentage of the world's gross national product was declining. In 1970 America produced about 30% of the world's goods and services; today, around 22%.

Henceforth the United States would have to live in a world of relative security, capable of reducing dangers but unable to banish them.[2]

To adopt this kind of line with respect to the place of the Suez Crisis in the story of British decline is, however, somewhat controversial. Consider, for example, the liquidation of the British Empire. There are some historians who hold that British withdrawal from much of Africa was by no means a well-managed adjustment to the inevitable but assumed, in the aftermath of Suez, an appearance of near-panic. 'The wind of change' (as Macmillan described it) was, according to this view, more like a hurricane, resulting in the British being evicted from the whole of Africa within a decade of Suez rather than over a protracted period that was otherwise the likely prognosis. An alternative interpretation involves placing stress on the argument that the sudden rise of nationalism in Black Africa owed little or nothing to Nasser's victory over Eden. The revolt against the colonialists and the white settlers – and not only the British were affected – had its roots in local conditions. Support for this contention is bolstered by reference to the records of Black African Liberation Movements and to the public speeches of their leaders: Suez rarely merits a mention. But a rejoinder to this argument runs that we should not overlook the unspoken assumptions that influence any generation of leaders: they are so much a part of the furniture of a period that elaborating them is simply rendered otiose.³ This controversy, then, is clearly set for a lengthy run.

The impact on the Middle East

It is likely to be much the same story in the matter of the impact of Suez on the Middle East itself. At one extreme is the view expressed by the American journalist Donald Neff. The very title of his book on Suez is revealing: *Warriors at Suez: Eisenhower Takes America into the Middle East*. He claims: 'Suez was a hinge point in history. It spelled the end of Western colonialism and the entry of America as the major Western power in the Middle East.' He also sees Great Britain, France and Israel as having decisively discredited themselves, thereby providing the opportunity for which the Soviets had been waiting:

Britain, France and Israel, by colluding and waging an unprovoked war, displayed such contempt for justice and the rule of law that they badly blotched the West's record in its competition against Communism. No longer, after Suez, could the West assert that it was uniquely to be trusted as the champion of man's aspirations for a just world.

The Soviet Union secured its presence in the Middle East after Suez. The pro-West Iraqi regime fell in 1958, and both Iraq and Syria – soon followed by Libya – imitated Nasser's example and turned to the Soviets for aid and arms. Though Soviet fortunes, like American, have had their share of ups and downs over the years ([Anwar] Sadat's expulsion of Russian advisers in 1972 was a blow to Moscow), the Russians now appear so embedded in the Middle East that it seems unrealistic to suppose that any settlement of the region's continuing turmoil could occur without active Soviet support. The very thing that Eden had hoped to accomplish, preventing the replacement of British influence by Russia, is now a fact in the Middle East.⁴

The extent to which Suez was such 'a hinge point in history' in the Middle East is, of course, contentious. First, there is the argument naturally favoured by Eden at the time and in his memoirs that it was indeed a hinge point but that it was *not* disastrous for Great Britain, France and Israel. On the contrary, it served decisively to check Nasser as Mussolini and

Hitler had not been checked in the 1930s. Nettled by a memorandum, dated 4 January 1957, in which Macmillan wrote that 'the Suez operation has been a tactical defeat', Eden in one of his last acts as Prime Minister presented the following written appraisal to his Cabinet colleagues:

I do not think that the events of Suez can be reckoned as a tactical defeat. It is much too early to pronounce on an operation of this kind.
    This much is certain:
    The Soviet Egyptian air force has been destroyed. The Israelis have eliminated one-third of the Egyptian army and its equipment.
    Jordan and Syria have been kept from active alignment with Nasser, whose personal position has not (according to our reports) been strengthened.
    The extent of Soviet penetration of the Middle East has been exposed, with the result that the United States at last seems to be taking the action for which we pleaded in vain throughout 1956 . . .[5]

Such arguments, unqualified by any admission of the negative aspects from the British standpoint, have the appearance of special pleading and they are thus unlikely to carry weight among historians. But a more balanced case was developed by Lloyd in his account of the crisis published in 1978. While conceding that 'there can be no disputing the fact that we sustained a diplomatic and political defeat', he saw some compensating gains in the Middle East. Above all, he rested his case on speculation about what was likely to have happened if no military intervention had taken place in 1956:

If the Middle East had seen him [Nasser] successfully defy the Western powers, his prestige would have been enormous. I believe that within a matter of months, not only would the regime of King Feisal, the Crown Prince, and Nuri have been overthrown in Iraq, but King Hussein too, would have been eliminated in Jordan. The same thing would have happened to King Idris in Libya and President [Camille] Chamoun would have been in grave danger in the Lebanon. The oil sheikdoms in the Gulf, incapable of defending themselves, would have been taken over by Nasser or his nominees. The oil problems of 1974 might have arisen many years earlier. The Sudan would also have been in danger. The royal house in Saudi Arabia would also have been undermined.[6]

There is indeed some merit in the argument that Nasser had been checked by what had happened. True, he and his followers throughout the Middle East could rejoice in the humiliation of the British and the French at the hands of the United Nations and, in particular, the United States. But the other less comfortable truth that had to be faced was that at the military level the Egyptians had been humiliated – at the hands not only of the Europeans but, more important, of the hated Israelis. To some extent this did puncture Egypt's prestige and may help to explain why the Nasserite Revolution in subsequent years made only patchy progress in the region as a whole.

As for the relative weight in the Middle East of the British, the Americans and the Soviets, it is again possible to maintain that Suez was not quite 'the hinge point of history' that Neff claimed. British influence in the region did *not* in fact collapse overnight following the Suez débâcle. True, pro-British regimes in Iraq and Libya were overturned during the ensuing decade. But pro-British regimes survived in Jordan and Kuwait, in both cases as a result of the timely despatch of British forces in 1958 and 1961 respectively. And Lloyd was probably correct in claiming that 'in 1964 we were certainly as powerful in the Persian Gulf as we had been in 1956.'[7] At all events, subsequent British withdrawal from 'East of Suez' by the Labour government of Harold Wilson was clearly not directly caused by the Suez Crisis but derived from a combination of the need to make financial savings and domestic Party considerations.

So far as the Americans were concerned, the Suez Crisis may likewise have been only one of a number of factors gradually leading them towards a greater degree of involvement in the Middle East. True, it may have precipitated the enunciation of the so-called Eisenhower Doctrine. This was a request by the President to the Congress, made on 5 January 1957, to provide additional economic and military assistance to nations in the region and for authorization to use American forces 'to secure and protect the territorial integrity and political independence of such nations, requesting such aid, against armed aggression from any nation controlled by International Communism'.[8]

Congress eventually concurred and one rather spectacular result was the despatch of American marines to the Lebanon in 1958. But the 'Eisenhower Doctrine' certainly did not mark the beginning of American involvement in the Middle East and hence was not really a dramatic break with the past. For example, the Americans, since the end of the Second World War, had had a special relationship with Saudi Arabia. Again, it had been the US Central Intelligence Agency, in association with the British, that had masterminded the pro-Western coup against Mussadiq in Iran in 1953. And the long-standing close American relationship with Israel needs no emphasis. Thus the Suez Crisis was probably a good deal less seminal in shaping long-term American policies in the Middle East than talk of a 'hinge point in history' would suggest. Much the same is probably also true for the Soviets. Their increasing involvement in the wider world – by no means limited to the Middle East – has been a major feature of the international scene since 1945 and it clearly has not been dependent on the events of a single year. Moreover, as has been seen, the Soviet role in supplying arms and advisers to Egypt had preceded the nationalization of the Suez Canal and this process was probably neither greatly slowed nor greatly advanced by the Anglo-French operation.

The Anglo-French divergence: NATO and the EEC

If the Suez Crisis had only limited long-term effects on the Middle East, could it be that it actually had more seminal consequences for NATO? The case for taking this line rests on the divergent courses taken by Great Britain and France during the ensuing decade and the importance that Suez may have had in causing this. In the case of France the argument runs that there was unusual dismay not only at American hostility to the operation but at the capitulation of the British in the face of American pressure. The eventual results may have been profoundly significant. The fact is that Eden informed rather than consulted Mollet on 6 November about the ceasefire decision and this led to assumptions being made in Paris that the British were, after all, mere subalterns in an Anglo-Saxon dominated Western security system. It was therefore probably not coincidental that on 5 December 1956 Mollet formally issued a decree creating a Committee for Military Applications of Atomic Energy. This put France on a path to acquiring a truly independent nuclear capability, something that nowadays has a remarkable degree of all-party support. Charles de Gaulle, who became Prime Minister in 1958 and President in 1959, reinforced this development but he did not pioneer it. As David S. Yost has written:

France's own research on nuclear weapons had been well under way even prior to 1956, when the Comité des Applications Militaires was established in the Commisariat à l'Energie Atomique (CEA). The Suez humiliation of 1956 was decisive in convincing the French leaders such as Prime Minister Guy Mollet of the political importance of exploiting the technological opportunity under development. It was felt that a nuclear weapons capability would reduce France's dependence on the US and her vulnerability to Soviet blackmail. Sentiments of dependence and vulnerability had been heightened by Suez, together with French determination to act. In late 1956 the Minister of the Armed Forces approved a programme of CEA research including preparatory studies for nuclear explosive tests and, depending on further government decisions, the construction of prototype weapons. This decision went further than the 1954 decision by [Pierre] Mendès-France to approve studies that would maintain France's nuclear weapons option, and furnished the basis for Prime Minister Félix Gaillard's decision in April 1958 to order France's first explosive test for 1960. The Fourth Republic (1946–58) thus prefigured de Gaulle.[9]

Later, under de Gaulle, France decisively set its face against seeking any American assistance with its independent nuclear weapons programme with the result that today the country is in no way vulnerable to any American pressures that might arise from a superpower-led drive to create a nuclear-free Europe. The French have also consistently refused to allow American nuclear weapons to be based on their territory (with happy results in terms of domestic consensus). And since 1966 France has effectively excluded itself from NATO's military structure.

In the case of Great Britain, entirely different policies were pursued in the aftermath of Suez. In Lloyd's judgement one 'rather odd result was that Suez led to closer co-operation between the British and the United States Governments'.[10] This was perhaps not such an odd outcome as he supposed. For the new Prime Minister, Macmillan, had been a direct beneficiary of the breakdown in Anglo-American relations under Eden. It is not perhaps surprising that, having intrigued behind Eden's back with the Americans, Macmillan once in 10 Downing Street should have been content to be little more than Eisenhower's subaltern on most major issues concerning Western security. During 1957, for example, he had two vital encounters with Eisenhower that effectively established a 'special nuclear relationship' between the United States and Great Britain. At a meeting in March in Bermuda the British agreed to 60 intermediate-range, land-based ballistic missiles, known as Thors, being deployed in East Anglia. And in a meeting in Washington in October Eisenhower offered, as a virtual *quid pro quo*, 'to request the Congress to amend the Atomic Energy Act of 1954 as may be necessary and desirable to permit close and fruitful collaboration of scientists and engineers of Great Britain, the United States and other friendly countries'.[11] In fact, because of attitudes then developing in Paris no other 'friendly country' ever materialized. Hence, in 1958 Great Britain and the United States signed the Agreement for Cooperation on Uses of Atomic Energy for Mutual Defence Purposes. John Baylis has written of its importance:

The significance of the agreement . . . was that it provided a continuing basis for wide-ranging nuclear collaboration between the two countries especially in the field of design and production of nuclear warheads which has continued through to the present day. As a result of the agreement Britain was able to design and produce smaller, more sophisticated warheads of her own which were needed firstly for the ill-fated Blue Streak missile and later for the American Polaris missile. In this field as a result of American assistance Britain has been able to retain an important lead over all the other nuclear medium powers.[12]

But that lead is today under challenge from France. Moreover, as stated, the advantages of any British lead has to be weighed against present and future costs of dependence on Washington for supplies of missiles and against the lack of domestic consensus that has been an inevitable concomitant of so close a defence relationship with a less than universally popular super-power.

The British also paid another price for becoming little more than auxiliaries to the Americans during Macmillan's premiership: in de Gaulle's time they were to be pointedly excluded from membership of the European Economic Community (EEC). The precise consequences of this prolonged absence are, of course, controversial and no attempt will be made here to evaluate them. But for our purposes we need to ask whether the exclusion was the *direct* result of the Suez Crisis. The point cannot be proved. For it is at least arguable that had Butler (or some other leading Conservative) succeeded Eden the extent of the deference paid to the Americans might have been a good deal less and the decision to forge a 'special nuclear relationship' with Washington might never have occurred. In that case, Great Britain might have been readily admitted to the EEC as early as 1963. If this thesis has merit, then the dramatic long-term divergence between Great Britain and France and British exclusion from the EEC was *not* the result of the Suez Crisis – not even the events of 6 November – but was the direct consequence of the course Macmillan voluntarily and enthusiastically charted *after* the Suez Crisis had ceased to be of central importance in the Anglo-American relationship.

The domestic impact

It may be, then, that the most permanent impact of the Suez Affair lay in the domestic arena. But here again there is scope for controversy. Consider, for example, the effect on the general public. According to Enoch Powell:

The Suez fiasco cut deep into the consciousness of the British people. It had the same sort of effect as a nervous breakdown, similar to what America experienced after the Vietnam war but more severe. They no longer felt sure of themselves. They disbelieved that they could any longer be a nation, with all that meant in terms of independence, pride and self-confidence.[13]

Perhaps so. But opinion polls did not reveal any deep or consistent disenchantment with the Conservative government during or even immediately after the Suez Crisis. And by-election results revealed only a slight increase in adverse swing against the Conservatives in the year after the Suez operation as the following table illustrates:

Three groups of by-elections of 1955–9 in which results can be compared with the 1955 General Election

Group	*Average (mean) Conservative loss in percentage of poll*
8 by-elections from 7 Dec. 1955 to 27 Sept. 1956	−4.4
8 by-elections from 15 Nov. 1956 to 28 Nov. 1957	−6.2
10 by-elections from 13 June 1958 to 18 June 1959	−3.6

Source: Leon D. Epstein, *British Politics in the Suez Crisis* (London, 1964), p. 151

By the standards of by-election patterns in all subsequent Parliaments to date, these were modest swings indeed. Moreover, the Conservatives in the General Election of 1959 greatly increased their overall majority in the House of Commons from 60 to 100. All this certainly does not prove that Suez actually helped the Conservatives, for Labour did not see fit to place the issue at the centre of its election campaigning. But it is clearly even more difficult to argue the opposite case. In short, Suez probably made little difference to most ordinary electors' political preferences.

Where Suez may have been of more importance lay in the impact on the political activists in the two main parties. Let us first consider the Conservative Party. The most striking effect was probably that on the MPs in the 'Suez Group' and those who had leaned in their direction in times of crisis. All but a small minority of these MPs and their supporters in the broader Conservative Party seem to have drawn the conclusion that 'gunboat diplomacy' was ceasing to be practical politics. And, as a result, Macmillan had little difficulty in pursuing policies that greatly accelerated the rate of decolonization. Again, most Conservative backbenchers and activists soon adjusted to the need to forgive the Americans for their hostility to the Suez operation. True, in the immediate aftermath of the ceasefire as many as 127 Conservative MPs signed a Commons motion criticizing the United States for 'gravely endangering the Atlantic Alliance'. But once Macmillan had become Prime Minister almost no resistance to his extremely pro-American policies was offered. In short, the retirement of Eden had left putative British 'Gaullism' without a leader and hence anti-Americanism became thereafter a near-monopoly of the Left. But again it is debatable whether this outcome owed more to the Suez débâcle or to Macmillan's personal predilections.

So far as the Labour Party was concerned, it would seem that the Suez Affair greatly strengthened anti-imperialist sentiment among MPs and activists. But, as more than one writer has noted, the most striking result was the emergence on the British Left of a peculiarly inverted form of jingoism. Leon D. Epstein commented as early as 1964:

A significant aspect of this well-known anti-imperialist attitude was that its exponents also believed in the continued greatness of the British role in the world. Forcible domination of other countries was rejected, to be sure, but for this traditional basis for British influence the anti-imperialists almost always sought to substitute a new moral force that would be just as British as that which had gone before. As Earl Attlee said [on 13 September 1956], '... in these days Great Britain's influence in the world depends far more on moral leadership than on force.' Socialists argued that they were best equipped to supply this leadership, presumably because of their break from the nation's imperial past. The act of freeing colonial dependencies supplied a basis for 'giving a lead' to the rest of the world in standards of international morality. The paradox is that this very policy of moral leadership depended on Britain having an empire to surrender. Anti-imperialism required an imperialist past and present. Britain's claim to lead the world morally derived from the fact that it had recently led by other means. British leadership, in any form, through the new Commonwealth concept for example, was simply the last and least substantial of the old imperialist ideas of Britain's destiny in the world. The imperial experience thus left its mark on the attitudes of its critics as well as of its champions. Both, in the mid-twentieth century, hankered for a national greatness that had only recently seemed certain to be Britain's destiny.[14]

Robert Skidelsky wrote in similar vein in 1970:

If anything the Labour Party's illusion ran deeper. The Tories' concept of their post-imperial responsibilities rested upon the illusion of power. Once that illusion was shattered, little remained of that concept: the way was opened to joining Europe. But the Labour Party's illusion rested on something that no mere harsh facts could dispose of. The old imperialist idea had been transposed into a dream of world brotherhood. It rested on the repudiation of power, the repudiation, in fact, of everything that goes to make up the real world. It was imperialism with all the pain, the injustice, the cruelty and the oppression conjured out of existence by magic. It was the imperialism of the intelligentsia, both an atonement for past sins and a guarantee of status without tears.[15]

All Labour's leading figures were influenced to some extent by this kind of thinking. Deep divisions, however, were to arise on the British Left over the precise extent to which 'world brotherhood' and 'the repudiation of power' should be pursued given the presumed scepticism of the mass of Labour voters. Gaitskell drew the line at what he characterized as pacifism and neutralism. And he had a temporary success with his famous 'fight, fight and fight again' speech. But by the 1980s Labour had come to be led by Michael Foot and Neil Kinnock who seemed in many respects to be throwbacks to the heyday of inverted chauvinism. (Foot, of course, was an actual political survivor from the earlier period.) Whether their outlook contributed to Labour's catastrophic electoral defeats in 1983 and 1987 is debatable. But there is here a superficial contrast with François Mitterrand, the robust (and highly successful) leader of the French Socialists in the 1980s. Yet perhaps in a sense the British and French Socialist leaders represent two sides of the same coin in that neither believes in the almost unlimited deference to Washington that has been the hallmark of all post-Suez British premierships with the possible exception of that of Edward Heath.

Eden's reputation

It is probably appropriate to conclude with some reflections on Eden himself. For the long-term effect of Suez on his standing at the bar of history has been catastrophic. As one of his earlier biographers wrote: 'The reputation he had built since 1923 remains identified with one event – the Suez crisis. It is a cruel fate, even by the harsh standards of politics, to be remembered by one failure and not by numerous achievements.'[16] To another historian, indeed, 'he has become the scapegoat for the affair', whereas most of his Cabinet colleagues are now recalled not primarily for their part in Suez but for their subsequent deeds.[17] In this volume it has been argued that Eden was faced with unprecedented pressures which make it impossible not to feel a measure of sympathy for him. How could he, the heir to Churchill, simply meekly tolerate the stunning blow to British prestige deliberately and brutally inflicted by Nasser? Yet how could he act decisively in the face of American hostility and of a divided Cabinet (some of whose members appear to have been more than usually tempted to serve their own career interests by contemplating disloyalty to their chief)? In short, so far as taking action against Nasser was concerned, he was probably damned if he did and damned if he didn't.

Yet sympathy for Eden can only be taken so far. For his conduct during his two decades in retirement – he died only in January 1977 – reveals that he himself partially recognized that by most normal standards he had behaved dishonourably in entering into a conspiracy with the French and the Israelis and then in subsequently telling lies about it in Parliament. Nor did he ever publicly acknowledge let alone apologize for these lies. For example, his memoirs of the Suez Affair, published in *Full Circle*, were notable for his total unwillingness to face up to the collusion issue. Yet because they appeared as early as 1960 some may be inclined to excuse him for such *suppressio veri*. What cannot be so charitably explained, however, is his continuing silence on the matter for the remainder of his life, even though the broad facts about the Sèvres meetings had become public knowledge by the mid-1960s. Often interviewed by authors, journalists and broadcasters about his career as a whole, he consistently avoided or evaded questions about collusion. Had he wished to face up to the challenge he could, of course, easily have created a suitable opportunity. His failure to do so reveals a sense of unease that posterity will surely not be able to ignore.

Posterity may also be especially fascinated by what happened on 4 November 1956. As has been seen, Eden and his colleagues were faced with indications that the Israelis had agreed to a ceasefire and hence had arguably undermined the case for Anglo-French forces proceeding with the invasion of Egypt. Until the reports were shown to be false, Eden and his colleagues were painfully divided as to how to react. In short, such was the pass to which Great Britain had been reduced that its leaders could not even decide whether or not they had been hoist with their own petard. Peace or war with one Third World country, then, may have rested on whether another Third World country would renege on the spirit of a disreputable collusive bargain. This was surely a moment of deep humiliation for a supposedly great power and a supposedly great statesman. But what followed may have been worse. For, as Eden's widow's diary reveals, news that Israel was not in fact accepting a ceasefire produced a scene that must rank in drama with any that the British Cabinet room has seen: 'Everyone laughed and banged the table with relief except Birch and Monckton who looked glum.'[18]

Those present were for the most part men of considerable private wealth from the best families in the land; most were declared Christians; many had fought gallantly in world wars against front-rank adversaries; and most had attended prominent public schools where they would inevitably have been raised on the ethical values of *Tom Brown's Schooldays*. Yet here they were raucously rejoicing that a decision by a handful of Jews would after all enable them to bombard and invade Port Said and continue to bomb Cairo. Many poverty-stricken Egyptians would thereby be enabled to meet their deaths accompanied by high-minded British pieties about separating combatants. It cannot surely be doubted that the shade of Flashman would have been among the laughing table-bangers.

What is less certain is whether, in the desperate plight to which his country had been reduced, he would also have been joined in this act of apparent collective rottenness by the shade of Tom Brown himself. At all events, this was surely a moment of truth in the British story – not least for Eden. As his obiturist put it in *The Times* in 1977: 'He was the last Prime Minister to believe Britain was a great power and the first to confront a crisis which proved she was not.'[19]

Notes

1 David Carlton, *Anthony Eden: a Biography* (London, 1981), p. 478.
2 *The Sunday Times*, 18 November 1984.
3 Arguments and counter-arguments along these lines are to be found in Anthony Low and Brian Lapping, 'Controversy: did Suez hasten the end of Empire?', *Contemporary Record*, vol. 1, no. 2 (summer 1987), pp. 31–3; and Robert Holland, 'Controversy: did Suez hasten the end of Empire?', *Contemporary Record*, vol. 1, no. 4 (winter 1988), p. 39.
4 Donald Neff, *Warriors at Suez: Eisenhower Takes America into the Middle East* (New York, 1981), pp. 438–9.
5 Cab. 129/84, PRO.
6 Selwyn Lloyd, *Suez 1956: a Personal Account* (London, 1978), p. 259.
7 Ibid., p. 257.
8 Stephen Ambrose, *Eisenhower: the President 1952–1969* (London, 1984), p. 382.
9 David S. Yost, *France's Deterrent Posture and Security in Europe*, International Institute for Strategic Studies Adelphi Papers nos. 194 and 195 (London, 1984–85), no. 194, p. 4.
10 Lloyd, *Suez 1956*, p. 257.
11 John Baylis, *Anglo-American Defence Relations, 1939–1984: the Special Relationship* (2nd edn, London, 1984), p. 90.
12 Ibid., p. 91.
13 Enoch Powell, 'The death of Britain', *The Times*, 13 October 1987.
14 Leon D. Epstein, *British Politics in the Suez Crisis* (London, 1964), pp. 28–9.
15 Robert Skidelsky, 'Lessons of Suez', in Vernon Bogdanor and Robert Skidelsky (eds), *The Age of Affluence, 1951–1964* (London, 1970), pp. 188–9.

16 Sidney Aster, *Anthony Eden* (London, 1976), p. 165.
17 Richard Lamb, *The Failure of the Eden Government* (London, 1987), p. viii.
18 See chapter 4, n. 35.
19 Quoted in Neff, *Warriors at Suez*, p. 437.

Appendix I

Excerpts from the Private Correspondence of Eden and Eisenhower during the Suez Crisis

Eden to Eisenhower, 27 July 1956

This morning I have reviewed the whole position with my Cabinet colleagues and Chiefs of Staff. We are all agreed that we cannot afford to allow Nasser to seize control of the Canal in this way, in defiance of international agreements. If we take a firm stand over this now, we shall have the support of all the maritime powers. If we do not, our influence and yours throughout the Middle East will, we are all convinced, be finally destroyed.

The immediate threat is to the oil supplies to Western Europe, a great part of which flows through the Canal. We have reserves in the United Kingdom which would last us for six weeks; and the countries of Western Europe have stocks, rather smaller as we believe, on which they could draw for a time. We are, however, at once considering means of limiting current consumption so as to conserve our supplies; and if the Canal were closed we should have to ask you to help us by reducing the amount which you draw from the pipeline terminals in the Eastern Mediterranean and possibly by sending us supplementary supplies for a time from your side of the world.

It is, however, the outlook for the longer term which is more threatening. The Canal is an international asset and facility, which is vital to the free world. The maritime Powers cannot afford to allow Egypt to expropriate it and to exploit it by using the revenues for her own internal purposes irrespective of the interests of the Canal and of the Canal users. Apart from the Egyptians' complete lack of technical qualifications, their past behaviour gives no confidence that they can be trusted to manage it with any sense of international obligation. Nor are they capable of providing the capital which will soon be needed to widen and deepen it so that it may be capable of handling the increased volume of traffic which it must carry in the years to come. We should, I am convinced, take this opportunity to put its management on a firm and lasting basis as an international trust.

We should not allow ourselves to become involved in legal quibbles about the rights of the Egyptian Government to nationalize what is technically an Egyptian company, or in financial arguments about their capacity to pay the compensation which they have offered. I feel sure that we should take issue with Nasser on the broader international grounds . . .

As we see it we are unlikely to attain our objectives by economic pressures alone. I gather that Egypt is not due to receive any further aid from you. No large payments from her sterling balances here are due before January. We ought in the first instance to bring the maximum political pressure to bear on Egypt. For this, apart from our own action, we should invoke the support of all the interested Powers. My colleagues and I are convinced that we must be ready, in the last resort, to use force to bring Nasser to his senses. For our part we are prepared to do so. I have this morning instructed our Chiefs of Staff to prepare a military plan accordingly.

However, the first step must be for you and us and France to exchange views, align our policies and concert together how we can best bring the maximum pressure to bear on the Egyptian Government.

Eisenhower to Eden, 31 July 1956

From the moment that Nasser announced nationalization of the Suez Canal Company, my thoughts have been constantly with you. Grave problems are placed before both our governments, although for each of us they naturally differ in type and character. Until this morning, I was happy to feel that we were approaching decisions as to applicable procedures somewhat along parallel lines, even though there were, as would be expected, important differences as to detail. But early this morning I received the messages, communicated to me through Murphy from you and Harold Macmillan, telling me on a most secret basis of your decision to employ force without delay or attempting any intermediate and less drastic steps.

We recognize the transcendent worth of the Canal to the free world and the possibility that eventually the use of force might become necessary in order to protect international rights. But we have been hopeful that through a Conference in which would be represented the signatories to the Convention of 1888, as well as other maritime nations, there would be brought about such pressures on the Egyptian government that the efficient operation of the Canal could be assured for the future.

For my part, I cannot over-emphasize the strength of my conviction that some such method must be attempted before action such as you contemplate should be undertaken. If unfortunately the situation can finally be resolved only by drastic means, there should be no grounds for belief anywhere that corrective measures were undertaken merely to protect national or individual investors, or the legal rights of a sovereign nation were ruthlessly flouted. A conference, at the very least, should have a great educational effect throughout the world. Public opinion here and, I am convinced, in most of the world, would be outraged should there be a failure to make such efforts. Moreover, initial military successes might be easy, but the eventual price might become far too heavy.

I have given you my own personal conviction, as well as that of my associates, as to the unwisdom even of contemplating the use of military force at this moment. Assuming, however, that the whole situation continued to deteriorate to the point where such action would seem the only recourse, there are certain political facts to remember. As you realize, employment of United States forces is possible only through positive action on the part of the Congress, which is now adjourned but can be reconvened on my call for special reasons. If those reasons should involve the issue of employing United States military strength abroad, there would have to be a showing that every peaceful means of resolving the difficulty had previously been exhausted. Without such a showing, there would be a reaction that could very seriously affect our peoples' feeling toward our Western Allies. I do not want to exaggerate, but I assure you that this could grow to such an intensity as to have the most far-reaching consequences.

I realize that the messages from both you and Harold stressed that the decision taken was already approved by the government and was firm and irrevocable. But I personally feel sure that the American reaction would be severe and that the great areas of the world would share that reaction. On the other hand, I believe we can marshal that opinion in support of a reasonable and conciliatory, but absolutely firm, position. So I hope that you will consent to reviewing this matter once more in its broadest aspects. It is for this reason that I have asked

Foster to leave this afternoon to meet with your people tomorrow in London.

I have given you here only a few highlights in the chain of reasoning that compels us to conclude that the step you contemplate should not be undertaken until every peaceful means of protecting the rights and the livelihood of great portions of the world had been thoroughly explored and exhausted. Should these means fail, and I think it is erroneous to assume in advance that they needs must fail, then world opinion would understand how earnestly all of us had attempted to be just, fair and considerate, but that we simply could not accept a situation that would in the long run prove disastrous to the prosperity and living standards of every nation whose economy depends directly or indirectly upon East–West shipping.

With warm personal regard – and with earnest assurances of my continuing respect and friendship.

Eden to Eisenhower, 5 August 1956

... I do not think that we disagree about our primary objective ... to undo what Nasser has done and to set up an International Regime for the Canal ... But this is not all. Nasser has embarked on a course which is unpleasantly familiar ...

I have never thought Nasser a Hitler ... But the parallel with Mussolini is close. Neither of us can forget the lives and treasure he cost us before he was finally dealt with.

The removal of Nasser, and the installation in Egypt of a regime less hostile to the West, must therefore also rank high among our objectives. We must hope, as you say in your message, that the forthcoming conference will bring such pressures upon Nasser that the efficient operation of the Canal can be assured for the future. If so, everyone will be relieved and there will be no need of force. Moreover, if Nasser is compelled to disgorge his spoils, it is improbable that he will be able to maintain his internal position. We should thus have achieved our secondary objective ...

Our people here are neither excited nor eager to use force. They are, however, grimly determined that Nasser shall not get away with it this time, because they are convinced that if he does their existence will be at his mercy. So am I. ...

Eden to Eisenhower, 27 August 1956

This is a message to thank you for all the help Foster has given. Though I could not be at the Conference myself, I heard praise on all sides for the outstanding quality of his speeches and his constructive leadership. He will tell you how things have gone. It was, I think, a remarkable achievement to unite eighteen nations on an agreed statement of this clarity and force.

Before he left, Foster spoke to me of the destructive efforts of the Russians at the Conference. I have been giving some thought to this and I would like to give you my conclusions.

I have no doubt that the Bear is using Nasser, with or without his knowledge, to further his immediate aims. These are, I think, first to dislodge the West from the Middle East, and second to get a foothold in Africa so as to dominate that continent in turn. In this connection I have seen a reliable report from someone who was present at the lunch which Shepilov gave for the Arab Ambassadors. There the Soviet claim was that they 'only wanted to see Arab unity in Asia and Africa and the abolition of all foreign bases and exploitation. An agreed unified Arab nation must take its rightful place in the world.'

This policy is clearly aimed at Wheelus Field and Habbaniya, as well as at our Middle East oil supplies. Meanwhile the Communist bloc continue their economic and political blandishments towards the African countries which are already independent. Soon they will have a wider field for subversion as our colonies, particularly in the West, achieve self-government. All this makes me more than ever sure that Nasser must not be allowed to get away with it this time. We have many friends in the Middle East and in Africa and others who are shrewd enough to know where the plans of a Nasser or a Musaddiq would lead them. But they will not be strong enough to stand against the power of the mobs if Nasser wins again. The firmer the front we show together, the greater the chance that Nasser will give way without the need for any resort to force. That is why we were grateful for your policy and Foster's expression of it at the Conference. It is also one of the reasons why we have to continue our military preparations in conjunction with our French allies.

We have been examining what other action could be taken if Nasser refuses to negotiate on the basis of the London Conference. There is the question of dues. The Dutch and the Germans have already indicated that they will give support in this respect. The Dutch may even be taking action in the next few days. Then there is the question of currency and economic action. We are studying these with your people and the French in London and will be sending our comments soon. It looks as though we shall have a few days until Nasser gives Menzies his final reply. After that we should be in a position to act swiftly. Selwyn Lloyd is telegraphing to Foster about tactics, particularly in relation to United Nations.

Meanwhile I thought I should set out some of our reflections on the dangerous situation which still confronts us. It is certainly the most hazardous that our country has known since 1940.

I was glad to see such excellent photographic testimony of your growing health and abounding energy. That is the very best news for us all.

Eisenhower to Eden, 2 September 1956

I am grateful for your recent letter, and especially for your kind words on the role of the United States during the London Conference on the Suez Canal. I share your satisfaction at the large number of nations which thought as we do about the future operation of the Canal. In achieving this result we have set in motion a force which I feel will be very useful to us – the united and clearly expressed opinion of the majority users of the Suez waterway and of those nations most dependent upon it. This will exert a pressure which Nasser can scarcely ignore. From Foster I know that this accomplishment is due in no small measure to the expert leadership exhibited by Selwyn Lloyd as Chairman of the Conference, and to the guidance which he received from you.

As for the Russians, it is clear that they sought, at London, to impede the consolidation of a majority point of view, and to generate an atmosphere in the Near East which would make it impossible for Nasser to accept our proposals. I entirely agree with you that the underlying purpose of their policy in this problem is to undermine the Western position in the Near East and Africa, and to weaken the Western nations at home. We must never lose sight of this point.

Now that the London Conference is over, our efforts must be concentrated on the successful outcome of the conversations with Nasser. This delicate situation is going to require the highest skill, not only on the part of the five-nation Committee but also on the part of our Governments. I share your view that it is important that Nasser be under no misapprehension as to the firm interest of the nations primarily concerned with the Canal in safeguarding their rights in that waterway.

As to the possibility of later appeal to the United Nations, we can envisage a situation which would require UN consideration and of course there should be no thought of military action before the influences of the UN are fully explored. However, and most important, we believe that, before going to the UN, the Suez Committee of Five should first be given full opportunity to carry out the course of action agreed upon in London, and to gauge Nasser's intentions.

If the diplomatic front we present is united and is backed by the overwhelming sentiment of our several peoples, the chances should be greater that Nasser will give way without the need for any resort to force. This belief explains our policy at the Conference and also explains the statement which I gave out through Foster after I got back from San Francisco and had a chance to talk fully with him.

I am afraid, Anthony, that from this point onward our views on this situation diverge. As to the use of force or the threat of force at this juncture, I continue to feel as I expressed myself in the letter Foster carried to you some weeks ago. Even now military preparations and civilian evacuation exposed to public view seem to be solidifying support for Nasser which has been shaky in many important quarters. I regard it as indispensable that if we are to proceed solidly together to the solution of this problem, public opinion in our several countries must be overwhelming in its support. I must tell you frankly that American public opinion flatly rejects the thought of using force, particularly when it does not seem that every possible peaceful means of protecting our vital interests has been exhausted without result. Moreover, I gravely doubt we could here secure Congressional authority even for the lesser support measures for which you might have to look to us.

I really do not see how a successful result could be achieved by forcible means. The use of force would, it seems to me, vastly increase the area of jeopardy. I do not see how the economy of Western Europe can long survive the burden of prolonged military operations, as well as the denial of Near East oil. Also the peoples of the Near East and of North Africa and, to some extent, of all of Asia and all of Africa, would be consolidated against the West to a degree which, I fear, could not be overcome in a generation and, perhaps not even in a century particularly having in mind the capacity of the Russians to make mischief. Before such action were undertaken, all our peoples should unitedly understand that there were no other means available to protect our vital rights and interests.

We have two problems, the first of which is the assurance of permanent and efficient operation of the Suez Canal with justice to all concerned. The second is to see that Nasser shall not grow as a menace to the peace and vital interests of the West. In my view, these two problems need not and possibly cannot be solved simultaneously and by the same methods, although we are exploring further means to this end.

The first is the most important for the moment and must be solved in such a way as not to make the second more difficult. Above all, there must be no grounds for our several peoples to believe that anyone is using the Canal difficulty as an excuse to proceed forcibly against Nasser. And we have friends in the Middle East who tell us they would like to see Nasser's deflation brought about. But they seem unanimous in feeling that the Suez is not the issue on which to attempt to do this by force. Under those circumstances, because of the temper of their population, they say they would have to support Nasser even against their better judgment.

Seldom, I think, have we been faced by so grave a problem. For the time being we must, I think, put our faith in the processes already at work to bring Nasser peacefully to accept the solution along the lines of the 18-nation proposals. I believe that even though this procedure may fail to give the setback to Nasser that he so much deserves, we can better retrieve our position subsequently than if military force were hastily invoked.

Of course, our departments are looking into the implications of all future developments. In this they will keep in close touch with appropriate officials of your Government, as is my wish.

Eden to Eisenhower, 6 September 1956

Thank you for your message and writing thus frankly.

There is no doubt as to where we are agreed and have been agreed from the very beginning, namely that we should do everything we can to get a peaceful settlement. It is in this spirit that we favoured calling the twenty-two power conference and that we have worked in the closest co-operation with you about this business since. There has never been any question of our suddenly or without further provocation resorting to arms, while these processes were at work. In any event, as your own wide knowledge would confirm, we could not have done this without extensive preparation lasting several weeks.

This question of precautions has troubled me considerably and still does. I have not forgotten the riots and murders in Cairo in 1952, for I was in charge here at the time when Winston was on the high seas on his way back from the US.

We are both agreed that we must give the Suez Committee every chance to fulfil their mission. This is our firm resolve. If the Committee and subsequent negotiations succeed in getting Nasser's agreement to the London proposals of the eighteen powers, there will be no call for force. But if the Committee fails, we must have some immediate alternative which will show that Nasser is not going to get his way. In this connection we are attracted by Foster's suggestion, if I understand it rightly, for the running of the canal by the users in virtue of their rights under the 1888 Convention. We heard about this from our Embassy in Washington yesterday. I think that we could go along with this, provided that the intention was made clear by both of us immediately the Menzies mission finishes its work. But unless we can proceed with this, or something very like it, what should the next step be?

You suggest that this is where we diverge. If that is so I think that the divergence springs from a difference in our assessment of Nasser's plans and intentions. May I set out our view of the position.

In the 1930s Hitler established his position by a series of carefully planned movements. These began with occupation of the Rhineland and were followed by successive acts of aggression against Austria, Czechoslovakia, Poland and the West. His actions were tolerated and excused by the majority of the population of Western Europe. It was argued either that Hitler had committed no act of aggression against anyone, or that he was entitled to do what he liked in his own territory, or that it was impossible to prove that he had any ulterior designs, or that the Covenant of the League of Nations did not entitle us to use force and that it would be wiser to wait until he did commit an act of aggression.

In more recent years Russia has attempted similar tactics. The blockade of Berlin was to have been the opening move in a campaign designed at least to deprive the Western powers of their whole position in Germany. On this occasion we fortunately reacted at once with the result that the Russian design was never unfolded. But I am sure that you would agree that it would be wrong to infer from this circumstance that no Russian design existed.

Similarly the seizure of the Suez Canal is, we are convinced, the opening gambit in a planned campaign designed by Nasser to expel all Western influence and interests from Arab countries. He believes that if he can get away with this, and if he can successfully defy eighteen nations, his prestige in Arabia will be so great that he will be able to mount revolutions of young officers in Saudi Arabia, Jordan, Syria and Iraq. (We know that he is already preparing a revolution in Iraq, which is most stable and progressive.) These new Governments will in effect be Egyptian satellites if not Russian ones. They will have to place their united oil resources under the control of a United Arabia led by Egypt and under Russian influence. When that moment comes Nasser can deny oil to Western Europe and we here shall all be at his mercy.

There are some who doubt whether Saudi Arabia, Iraq and Kuwait will be prepared even for a time to sacrifice their oil revenues for the sake of Nasser's ambitions. But if we place ourselves in their position I think the dangers are clear. If Nasser says to them, 'I have nationalized the Suez Canal. I have successfully defied eighteen powerful nations including the United States, I have defied the whole of the United Nations in the matter of the Israel blockade, I have expropriated all Western property. Trust me and withhold oil from Western Europe. Within six months or a year, the continent of Europe will be on its knees before you.' Will the Arabs not be prepared to follow this lead? Can we rely on them to be more sensible than were the Germans? Even if the Arabs eventually fall apart again as they did after the early Caliphs, the damage will have been done meanwhile.

In short we are convinced that if Nasser is allowed to defy the eighteen nations it will be a matter of months before revolution breaks out in the oil-bearing countries and the West is wholly deprived of Middle Eastern oil. In this belief we are fortified by the advice of friendly leaders in the Middle East.

The Iraqis are the most insistent in their warnings; both Nuri and the Crown Prince have spoken to us several times of the consequences of Nasser succeeding in his grab. They would be swept away. Other warnings have been given by the Shah to our Ambassador when he said that he gave getting rid of Nasser a very high priority. The Libyan Ambassador here, who was formerly Prime Minister, said that wise men must see the danger of Nasser succeeding. King Saud, of whose advice you will know more than we do, also spoke in apprehension to Prince Zaid of Iraq when he was there the other day. He said that it would be bad if Nasser emerged triumphant, for he agreed that Nasser's ambition was to become the Napoleon of the Arabs and if he succeeded the regimes in Iraq and Saudi Arabia would be swept away.

The difference which separates us today appears to be a difference of assessment of Nasser's plans and intentions and of the consequences in the Middle East of military action against him.

You may feel that even if we are right it would be better to wait until Nasser has unmistakably unveiled his intentions. But this was the argument which prevailed in 1936 and which we both rejected in 1948. Admittedly there are risks in the use of force against Egypt now.

It is, however, clear that military intervention designed to reverse Nasser's revolutions in the whole continent would be a much more costly and difficult undertaking. I am very troubled, as it is, that if we do not reach a conclusion either way about the Canal very soon one or other of these Eastern lands may be toppled at any moment by Nasser's revolutionary movements.

I agree with you that prolonged military operations as well as the denial of Middle East oil would place an immense strain on the economy of Western Europe. I can assure you that we are conscious of the burdens and perils attending military intervention. But if our assessment is correct, and if the only alternative is to allow Nasser's plans quietly to develop until this country and all Western Europe are held to ransom by Egypt acting at Russia's behest it seems to us that our duty is plain. We have many times led Europe in the fight for freedom. It would be an ignoble end to our long history if we tamely accepted to perish by degrees.

Eisenhower to Eden, 8 September 1956

Whenever, on any international question, I find myself differing even slightly from you, I feel a deep compulsion to re-examine my position instantly and carefully. But permit me to suggest that when you use phrases in connection with the Suez affair, like 'ignoble end to our long history' in describing the possible future of your great country, you are making Nasser a much more important figure than he is.

We have a grave problem confronting us in Nasser's reckless adventure with the Canal, and I do *not* differ from you in your estimate of his intentions and purposes. The place where we apparently do not agree is on the probable effects in the Arab world of the various possible reactions by the Western world.

You seem to believe that any long, drawn-out controversy either within the 18-nation group or in the United Nations will inevitably make Nasser an Arab hero and seriously damage the prestige of Western Europe, including the United Kingdom, and that of the United States. Further you apparently believe that there would soon result an upheaval in the Arab nations out of which Nasser would emerge as the acknowledged leader of Islam. This, I think, is a picture too dark and is severely distorted.

I shall try to give you a somewhat different appraisal of the situation. First, let me say that my own conclusions are based to some degree upon an understanding of current Arab feeling that differs somewhat from yours. I believe that as this quarrel now stands before the world, we can expect the Arabs to rally firmly to Nasser's support in either of two eventualities.

The first of these is that there should be a resort to force without thoroughly exploring and exhausting every possible peaceful means of settling the issue, regardless of the time consumed, and when there is no evidence before the world that Nasser intends to do more than to nationalize the Canal Company. Unless it can be shown to the world that he is an actual aggressor, then I think all Arabs would be forced to support him, even though some of the ruling monarchs might very much like to see him toppled.

The second would be what seemed like a capitulation to Nasser and complete acceptance of his rule of the Canal traffic.

The use of military force against Egypt under present circumstances might have consequences even more serious than causing the Arabs to support Nasser. It might cause a serious misunderstanding between our two countries because I must say frankly that there is as yet no public opinion in this country which is prepared to support such a move, and the most significant public opinion that there is seems to think that the United Nations was formed to prevent this very thing.

It is for reasons such as these that we have viewed with some misgivings your preparations for mounting a military expedition against Egypt. We believe that Nasser may try to go before the United Nations claiming that these actions imply a rejection of the peaceful machinery of settling the dispute, and therefore may ask the United Nations to brand these operations as aggression.

At the same time, we do not want any capitulation to Nasser. We want to stand firmly with you to deflate the ambitious pretensions of Nasser and to assure permanent free and effective use of the Suez waterway under the terms of the 1888 Treaty.

It seems to Foster and to me that the result that you and I both want can best be assured by slower and less dramatic processes than military force. There are many areas of endeavor which are not yet fully explored because exploration takes time.

We can, for example, promote a semi-permanent organization of the user governments to take over the greatest practical amount of the technical problems of the Canal, such as pilotage, the organization of the traffic patterns, and the collection of dues to cover actual expenses. This organization would be on the spot and in constant contact with Egypt and might work out a *de facto* 'coexistence' which would give the users the rights which we want.

There are economic pressures which, if continued, will cause distress in Egypt.

There are Arab rivalries to be exploited and which can be exploited if we do not make Nasser an Arab hero.

There are alternatives to the present dependence upon the Canal and pipelines which should be developed perhaps by more tankers, a possible new pipeline to Turkey and some possible re-routing of oil, including perhaps more from this hemisphere, particularly to European countries which can afford to pay for it in dollars.

Nasser thrives on drama. If we let some of the drama go out of the situation and concentrate upon the task of deflating him through slower but sure processes such as I described, I believe the desired results can more probably be obtained.

Gradually it seems to me we could isolate Nasser and gain a victory which would not only be bloodless, but would be more far-reaching in its ultimate consequences than could be anything brought about by force of arms. In addition, it would be less costly both now and in the future.

Of course, if during this process Nasser himself resorts to violence in clear disregard of the 1888 Treaty, then that would create a new situation and one in which he and not we would be violating the United Nations Charter.

I assure you we are not blind to the fact that eventually there may be no escape from the use of force. Our resolute purpose must be to create conditions of operation in which all users can have confidence. But to resort to military action when the world believes there are other means available for resolving the dispute would set in motion forces that could lead, in the years to come, to the most distressing results.

Obviously there are large areas of agreement between us. But in these exchanges directed towards differing methods I gain some clarification of the confusing and conflicting considerations that apply to this problem.

Eisenhower to Eden, 30 October 1956 (first telegram)

I address you in this note not only as head of Her Majesty's Government but as my long-time friend who has, with me, believed in and worked for real Anglo-American understanding.

Last night I invited Mr Coulson, currently your Washington representative to come to my house to talk over the worsening situation in the Middle East. I have no doubt that the gist of our conversation has already been communicated to you. But it seemed to me desirable that I should give you my impressions concerning certain phases of this whole affair that are disturbing me very much.

Without bothering here to discuss the military movements themselves and their possible grave consequences, I should like to ask your help in clearing up my understanding as to exactly what is happening between us and our European allies – especially between us, the French and yourselves.

We have learned that the French had provided Israel with a considerable amount of equipment, including airplanes, in excess of the amounts of which we were officially informed. This action was, as you know, in violation of agreements now existing between our three countries. We know also that this process has continued in other items of equipment.

Quite naturally we began watching with increased interest the affairs in the Eastern Mediterranean. Late last week we became convinced that the Israel mobilization was proceeding to a point where something more than mere defense was contemplated, and found the situation serious enough to send a precautionary note to Ben-Gurion. On Sunday we repeated this note of caution and made a public statement of our actions, informing both you and the French of our concern. On that day we discovered that the volume of communication traffic between Paris and Tel Aviv jumped enormously, alerting us to the probability that France and Israel were concerting detailed plans of some kind.

When on Monday actual military moves began, we quickly decided that the matter had to go immediately to the United Nations, in view of our Agreement of May, 1950, subscribed to by our three governments.

Last evening our Ambassador to the United Nations met with your Ambassador, Pierson Dixon, to request him to join us in presenting the case to the United Nations this morning. We were astonished to find that he was completely unsympathetic, stating frankly that his government would not agree to any action whatsoever to be taken against Israel. He further argued that the tripartite statement of May, 1950, was ancient history and without current validity.

All this development, with its possible consequences, including the possible involvement of you and the French in a general Arab war, seems to me to leave your government and ours in a very sad state of confusion, so far as any possibility of unified understanding and action are concerned. It is true that Egypt has not yet formally asked this government for aid. But the fact is that if the United Nations finds Israel to be an aggressor, Egypt could very well ask the Soviets for help

– and then the Middle East fat would really be in the fire. It is this latter possibility that has led us to insist that the West must ask for a United Nations examination and possible intervention, for we may shortly find ourselves not only at odds concerning what we should do, but confronted with a de facto situation that would make all our present troubles look puny indeed.

Because of all these possibilities, it seems to me of first importance that the UK and the US quickly and clearly lay out their present views and intentions before each other, and that, come what may, we find some way of concerting our ideas and plans so that we may not, in any real crisis, be powerless to act in concert because of misunderstanding of each other. I think it is important that our two peoples, as well as the French, have this clear understanding of our common or several viewpoints.

With warm personal regard.

Eden to Eisenhower, 30 October 1956 (first telegram)

I am sending you this hurried message to let you know at once how we regard the Israel–Egypt conflict. We have never made any secret of our belief that justice entitled us to defend our vital interests against Nasser's designs. But we acted with you in summoning the London Conference, in despatching the abortive Menzies mission and in seeking to establish SCUA. As you know, the Russians regarded the Security Council proceedings as a victory for themselves and Egypt. Nevertheless we continued through the Secretary-General of the United Nations to seek a basis for the continuation of the negotiations.

Now this has happened. When we received news of the Israel mobilization we instructed our Ambassador in Tel Aviv to urge restraint. Soon afterwards he sought and obtained an assurance that Israel would not attack Jordan. This seems to me important since it means that Israel will not enlarge the area of conflict or involve us in virtue of the Anglo-Jordan Treaty. In recent months we have several times warned the Israeli Government both publicly and privately that if they attacked Jordan we would honour our obligations. But we feel under no obligation to come to the aid of Egypt. Apart from the feelings of public opinion here Nasser and his Press have relieved us of any such obligation by their attitude to the Tripartite Declaration.

Egypt has to a large extent brought this attack on herself by insisting that the state of war persists, by defying the Security Council and by declaring her intention to marshal the Arab states for the destruction of Israel. The latest example of Egyptian intentions is the announcement of a joint command between Egypt, Jordan and Syria.

We have earnestly deliberated what we should do in this serious situation. We cannot afford to see the Canal closed or to lose the shipping which is daily on passage through it. We have a responsibility for the people in these ships. We feel that decisive action should be taken at once to stop hostilities. We have agreed with you to go to the Security Council and instructions are being sent this moment. Experience however shows that its procedure is unlikely to be either rapid or effective. . . .

Eisenhower to Eden, 30 October 1956 (second telegram)

This morning I sent you a long cable to say that we here felt very much in the dark as to your attitude and intentions with respect to the Middle East situation. I have just now received your cable on this subject for which I thank you very much. I shall be awaiting the further message to which you refer.

It seems obvious that your Government and ours hold somewhat different attitudes toward the Tripartite Declaration of 1950. Since we have never publicly announced any modification of the Declaration or any limitations upon its interpretation, we find it difficult at this moment to see how we can violate our pledged word.

In any event I shall earnestly and even anxiously watch the unfolding situation.

Eden to Eisenhower, 30 October 1956 (second telegram)

I undertook this morning to send you a further message immediately after we had met M. Mollet and M. Pineau.

It may be that Israel could be accused of a technical aggression. On the other hand for the reasons set forth in my earlier message we think that Israel has a case for arguing that she is acting in self-defence under the ever increasing pressure of certain Arab States led by Egypt. Nevertheless we would not wish to support or even condone the action of Israel. We consider that in view of the massive interests involved the first thing to do is to take effective and decisive steps to halt the fighting.

We have had to act quickly for time is short, and since there appears to be very little fighting up to now there is still a chance of preventing serious hostilities. Selwyn is giving a copy of the text of the declaration to Winthrop. I shall be announcing it this afternoon in the House of

Commons at 4.30 p.m. This is absolutely necessary since Parliament is sitting.

The purpose of the declaration is to make similar requests upon each party. First, that all hostilities by land and air should cease. Second, that the Canal Zone should be left free so that no fighting or incidents can take place there. But knowing what these people are, we felt it essential to have some kind of physical guarantees in order to secure the safety of the Canal. We are asking for Port Said and Ismailia and Suez. As the Israelites appear to be very near to Suez the requirement affects them as well as the Egyptians. We are emphasizing of course that this is to be a temporary measure pending a settlement of all these problems.

As I told you in my previous message, we entirely agree that this should go to the Security Council. But as you know well, the Council cannot move quickly in a critical position and we have felt it right to act, as it were, as trustees to protect our own interests and nationals. You may say we should wait until we are asked to move by the Security Council. But, of course, there could never be agreement on such a request.

Either side may refuse, in which case we shall take the necessary measures to enforce the declaration.

Now you will wonder why apart from the Security Council we have acted so promptly. Of course my first instinct would have been to ask you to associate yourself and your country with the declaration. But I know the constitutional and other difficulties in which you are placed. I think there is a chance that both sides will accept. In any case it would help this result very much if you found it possible to support what we have done at least in general terms. We are well aware that no real settlement of Middle Eastern problems is possible except through the closest cooperation between our two countries. Our two Governments have tried with the best will in the world all sorts of public and private negotiations through the last two or three years and they have all failed. This seems an opportunity for a fresh start.

I can assure you that any action which we may have to take to follow up the declaration is not part of a harking back to the old colonial and occupational concepts. We are most anxious to avoid this impression. Nothing could have prevented this volcano from erupting somewhere, but when the dust settles there may well be a chance for our doing a really constructive piece of work together and thereby strengthening the weakest point in the line against Communism.

It is a great grief to me that the events of the last few days have placed such a strain on the relations between our two countries. Of course I realise your feelings about the action which we felt compelled to take at such short notice. But if you will refer to my message of September 6, I think you will agree that what I said then has already begun to be confirmed by events.

I have always felt, as I made very clear to Mr Khrushchev, that the Middle East was an issue over which, in the last resort, we would have to fight.

I know that Foster thought we could have played this longer. But I am convinced that, if we had allowed things to drift, everything would have gone from bad to worse. Nasser would have become a kind of Moslem Mussolini and our friends in Iraq, Jordan, Saudi Arabia and even Iran would gradually have been brought down. His efforts would have spread westwards, and Libya and all North Africa would have been brought under his control. It may be that we might have obtained by negotiation a settlement of the Canal question which gave us a part of what we needed. But at best it would have taken a long time. Meanwhile Nasser would have been taking the tricks all round the Middle East. His last action in making a military command with Jordan and Syria was bound to provoke the Israelis, and of course it did so. They felt themselves imprisoned and naturally tried to break out. We were of course relieved that they broke in the direction of Egypt rather than of Jordan. But once they had moved, in whatever direction there was not a moment to be lost. We and the French were convinced that we had to act at once to forestall a general conflagration throughout the Middle East. And now that police action has been started it must be carried through. I am sure that this is the moment to curb Nasser's ambitions. If we let it pass, all of us will bitterly regret it. Here is our opportunity to secure an effective and final settlement of the problems of the Middle East. If we draw back now, chaos will not be avoided. Everything will go up in flames in the Middle East. You will realise, with all your experience, that we cannot have a military vacuum while a United Nations force is being constituted and is being transported to the spot. This is why we feel we must go on to hold the position until we can hand over the responsibility to the United Nations. If a barrier can be established in this way between the Arabs and the Israelis we shall then be strongly placed to call on the Israelis to withdraw. This in its turn will reduce the threat to the Canal and restore it to the general use of the world. By this means, we shall have taken the first step towards re-establishing authority in this area for our generation.

It is no mere form of words to say that we would be happy to hand over to an international organisation as soon as we possibly can. As you can imagine no-one feels more strongly about this than Harold who has to provide the money. We do not want occupation of Egypt, we could not afford it, and that is one of many other reasons why we got out of Suez two years ago.

I know how strongly you feel, as I do, the objections to the use of force, but this is not a situation which can be mended by words or resolutions. It is indeed ironical that at this very moment, when we are being pilloried as aggressors Russia is brutally reoccupying Hungary and threatening the whole of Eastern Europe, and no voice is raised in the United Nations in favour of intervention there. It may be that our two countries can take no practical action to redress that situation. But the Middle East is an area in which we could still take practical and effective action together.

I am sending you this message in the hope that you will at least understand the grievous decisions which we have had to make. I was deeply moved by your last message before our initial action, although I was not able to reply to it as I would have liked at the time.

After a few days you will be in a position to act with renewed authority. I beg you to believe what we are doing now will in our view facilitate your action. I would most earnestly ask you to put the great weight of your authority behind the proposal which we are now making to the United Nations.

I believe as firmly as ever that the future of all of us depends on the closest Anglo-American cooperation. It has of course been a grief to me to have had to make a temporary breach into it which I cannot disguise, but I know that you are a man of big enough heart and vision to take up things again on the basis of fact. If you cannot approve, I would like you at least to understand the terrible decisions that we have had to make. I remember nothing like them since the days when we were comrades together in the war. History alone can judge whether we have made the right decision, but I do want to assure you that we have made it from a genuine sense of responsibility, not only to our country, but to all the world.

Appendix II

**Excerpts from the British Cabinet Minutes,
27 July–6 November 1956**

27 July 1956

The Cabinet considered the situation created by the decision of the Egyptian Government to nationalise the Suez Canal Company.

The Prime Minister said that, with some of his senior colleagues, he had seen the French Ambassador and the United States Chargé d'Affaires on the previous evening and had informed them of the facts as we knew them. He had told them that Her Majesty's Government would take a most serious view of this situation and that any failure on the part of the Western Powers to take the necessary steps to regain control over the Canal would have disastrous consequences for the economic life of the Western Powers and for their standing and influence in the Middle East. The Cabinet should now consider what courses of action were open to us to safeguard our interests. Our first aim must be to reach a common understanding on the matter with the French, as our partners in the Canal enterprise, and with the United States Government. The French Foreign Minister, M. Pineau, was due to arrive in London on 29th July; and he proposed that he should send an urgent message to the President of the United States inviting him to send a representative to take part in discussions early in the following week.

The Cabinet were given the following information of the importance of the Suez Canal to trade and the flow of supplies, and of Egypt's financial position. . . .

The Cabinet next considered the legal position and the basis on which we could sustain, and justify to international opinion, a refusal to accept the decision of the Egyptian Prime Minister, Colonel Nasser, to nationalise the Canal.

The Cabinet agreed that we should be on weak ground in basing our resistance on the narrow argument that Colonel Nasser had acted illegally. The Suez Canal Company was registered as an Egyptian company under Egyptian law; and Colonel Nasser had indicated that he intended to compensate the shareholders at ruling market prices. From a narrow legal point of view, his action amounted to no more than a decision to buy out the shareholders. Our case must be presented on wider international grounds. Our argument must be that the Canal was an important international asset and facility, and that Egypt could not be allowed to exploit it for a purely internal purpose. The Egyptians had not the technical ability to manage it effectively; and their recent behaviour gave no confidence that they would recognise their international obligations in respect of it. Moreover, they would not be able to provide the resources needed for the capital development needed, in widening and deepening the Canal, to enable it to carry the increased volume of traffic which it should carry in the years ahead. The Canal was a vital link between the East and the West and its importance as an international waterway, recognised in the Convention signed in 1888, had increased with the development of the oil industry and the dependence of the world on oil supplies. It was not a piece of Egyptian property but an international asset of the highest importance and it should be managed as an international trust.

The Cabinet agreed that for these reasons every effort must be made to restore effective international control over the Canal. It was evident that the Egyptians would not yield to economic pressures alone. They must be subjected to the maximum political pressure which could be applied by the maritime and trading nations whose interests were most directly affected. And, in the last resort, this political pressure must be backed by the threat – and, if need be, the use – of force.

The Cabinet then considered the factors to be taken into account in preparing a plan of military operations against Egypt. In this part of the discussion the following points were made:–

(*a*) Egypt's military forces consisted mainly of three infantry divisions and one armoured division. She had about 500 tanks, and a great deal of armoured and wheeled equipment which was of doubtful efficiency. There were some 600–800 Polish and Czech technicians at present employed in the Egyptian Army, but it could not be predicted whether they would be willing to help the Egyptians in active operations. If they were, the Egyptian Army would be a more dangerous force. About two-thirds of the Egyptian forces were in the Sinai area; the armoured division, however, straddled the Canal.

(*b*) A military operation against Egypt, including consequential responsibilities for keeping the Canal in operation and controlling the area, would require the equivalent of three divisions. The necessary forces could be made available for this purpose; but, as a great quantity of vehicles and other heavy armoured equipment would have to be transported to the area by sea, the necessary preparations for mounting the operation would take several weeks. It would be necessary, moreover, to requisition ships and, possibly, to direct labour.

(*c*) While the military plan was being worked out, preparations would be made to build up a ring of bomber forces at points around Egypt. Fighter squadrons would also be sent to Cyprus. It would be a week before the full resources of Transport Command could be mobilised. The size of the air forces needed would depend on the type of bombing to be carried out.

(*d*) The naval forces available in the Mediterranean consisted of a carrier, a cruiser of the New Zealand Navy, 3 Daring Class destroyers, 7 destroyers and an amphibious warfare squadron. Another cruiser was approaching the Canal from the Red Sea; and, after discussion, it was agreed that she should be diverted to Aden. Summer leave in the Home Fleet was due to begin in the following week: it would be necessary to consider whether this should be stopped.

(*e*) In preparing any plan for military operations account must be taken of the possible effects on our Arab allies in the Middle East and the Persian Gulf if force were used against Egypt. It was important that the operations should be so planned as to reduce to the minimum the risk that other Arab States would be drawn into supporting Egypt.

(*f*) Consideration should be given to the possibility of cutting the oil pipeline from the Canal to Cairo, which was vital to the economic life of Egypt's capital.

The Prime Minister said that against this background the Cabinet must decide what our policy must be. He fully agreed that the question was not a legal issue but must be treated as a matter of the widest international importance. It must now be our aim to place the Suez Canal under the control of the Powers interested in international shipping and trade by means of a new international Commission on which Egypt would be given suitable representation. Colonel Nasser's action had presented us with an opportunity to find a lasting settlement of this problem, and we should not hesitate to take advantage of it. An interim note of protest against the decision to nationalise the Canal should be sent forthwith to the Egyptian Government and this should be followed up, as soon as possible, by more considered representations concerted with the Americans and the French. We should also consider inviting other maritime and trading countries to support this diplomatic pressure. Commonwealth Governments might suggest that the matter should be referred to the Security Council. He did not favour this course, which would expose us to the risk of a Soviet veto. It would be necessary, however, to consider denouncing the Canal Base Agreement of 1954 in view of the fact that Egypt had given an undertaking in this Agreement not to interfere with the Canal. The fundamental question before the Cabinet, however, was whether they were prepared in the last resort to pursue their objective by the threat or even the use of force, and whether they were ready, in default of assistance from the United States and France, to take military action alone.

The Cabinet agreed that our essential interests in this area must, if necessary, be safeguarded by military action and that the necessary preparations to this end must be made. Failure to hold the Suez Canal would lead inevitably to the loss one by one of all our interests and assets in the Middle East and, even if we had to act alone, we could not stop short of using force to protect our position if all other means of protecting it proved unavailing. . . .

28 August 1956

. . . The Cabinet then considered the political and economic consequences which would follow if Egypt's action in seizing the Suez Canal were allowed to pass uncorrected. Copies were produced of a paper (EC (56) 35) in which the Treasury had made a provisional assessment of the financial and economic considerations which were at stake. This showed that, if an atmosphere of crisis were avoided, the military precautions now in hand would not seriously disturb the equilibrium of the national economy, though they would tend to retard the progress which was being made in checking inflation and improving the balance of payments. If military operations had to be undertaken, the Budgetary cost would not be large in relation to the current level of defence expenditure, but more serious economic effects would flow from the dislocation of traffic through the Suez Canal. The major risk to the national economy lay in the threat to our oil supplies. If the Suez Canal were closed, the cost of obtaining oil from the Western Hemisphere to supplement our supplies would be a serious burden on our balance of payments and on our reserves of gold and dollars. If, in addition, the pipelines to the Levant were closed, we should be unable to obtain all the oil we needed, industry would be dislocated, and we should be unable to sustain for long the burden of paying for such oil supplies as we could obtain from the Western Hemisphere. If for any reason we also lost our oil supplies from the Persian Gulf, the economy of the United Kingdom and of Western Europe would cease to be viable.

The Chancellor of the Exchequer [Macmillan] said that our national economy now depended on supplies of oil from the Middle East. Colonel Nasser's ambitions threatened those supplies – directly, because they jeopardised the freedom and efficiency of the Suez Canal; and indirectly, because the success of his plans would inevitably impair our relations with the oil-producing countries of the Middle East.

In further discussion it was argued that, although those countries would still have an interest in selling their oil, it would not be satisfactory to us to be obliged to take it on their terms; and, as experience in Iran had shown, there could be no certainty that in these countries nationalist aspirations would not outweigh commercial self-interest. The Governors of Aden, Somaliland and Kenya had already given warning that the Arabs in those Colonies were watching for the outcome of this contest between Colonel Nasser and the Western Powers and that, if it ended in a triumph for Colonel Nasser, British influence among the Arabs in these countries would be destroyed. If this were true of Arab communities in British Colonial territories, it was evident that we should face a very serious situation in the Arab States themselves, and we could hardly hope to sustain for long our influence in Iraq or in the Persian Gulf. There could therefore be little doubt that, if Colonel Nasser's policy succeeded, our whole position in the Middle East would be undermined, our oil supplies would be in jeopardy, and the stability of our national economy would be gravely threatened.

The Minister of Defence [Monckton] said that, for the reasons which had been stated in the discussion, he agreed that we could not afford to allow Colonel Nasser to succeed in his attempt to seize control over the Suez Canal and that, if all other methods proved unavailing, force would have to be used to prevent it. On the other hand, the Cabinet should weigh the disadvantages of using force. If, together with the French, we took military measures against Egypt, our action would be condemned by a substantial body of public opinion in countries overseas, including several of the independent countries of the Commonwealth. Within the United Kingdom itself opinion would be divided. Our vital interests in other parts of the Middle East would also be affected; we must, in particular, expect sabotage against oil installations in other Arab countries. Moreover, once we had sent military forces into Egypt, it would not be easy to extricate them; we might find ourselves saddled with a costly commitment. While, therefore, he was ready to agree that we must continue to be prepared to use force in the last resort, he hoped that we should first exhaust all other means of curbing Colonel Nasser's ambitions and, in particular, that we should let no opportunity pass of securing a settlement by agreement.

11 September 1956

The Prime Minister, summing up this part of the discussion, said that it was evident that the Cabinet were in favour of proceeding with the plan for establishing an organisation to enable the principal users of the Canal to exercise their rights under the 1888 Convention, provided that the United States Government were willing that this project should be announced in the forthcoming debate in the House of Commons and brought into operation without delay; and that the Cabinet were further agreed that in this event, the situation should be formally notified to the Chairman of the Security Council under Article 35 of the United Nations Charter.

Discussion then turned on the further steps which might subsequently have to be taken.

The Chancellor of the Exchequer [Macmillan] said that, in his judgment, it was unlikely that effective international control over the Canal could be secured without the use of force. He regarded the establishment of this users' organisation as a step towards the ultimate use of force. It would not in itself provide a solution. It was very doubtful whether the Canal could be operated effectively under such an arrangement as this; and it seemed certain that the Egyptians could not accept it as a permanent system. It should, however, serve to bring the issue to a head. This was of great importance from the point of view of the national economy. If we could achieve a quick and satisfactory settlement of this issue, confidence in sterling would be restored; but, if a settlement was long delayed, the cost and the uncertainty would undermine our financial position. He therefore hoped that Parliament could be persuaded to give the Government a mandate to take all necessary steps, including the use of force, to secure a satisfactory settlement of this problem.

The Minister of Defence [Monckton] said that he hoped that the adoption of this plan for the establishment of a users' organisation would not be regarded solely as a step towards the use of force. He did not exclude the possibility that, if the Canal could be brought under effective international control, the present régime in Egypt might be overthrown by means short of war. Any premature recourse to force, especially without the support and approval of the United States, was likely to precipitate disorder throughout the Middle East and to alienate a substantial body of public opinion in this country and elsewhere throughout the world.

The Lord Chancellor [Kilmuir] said that it would be mistaken to assume that, if force had ultimately to be used, this would be inconsistent with the United Nations Charter. While the detailed provisions of the Charter placed all their emphasis on the preservation of peace, it was one of the essential purposes of the Charter, as reflected in the preamble, to secure respect for international obligations. It was this which was the main issue at stake in this situation. We certainly had a duty to do out utmost to secure it by peaceful means. The establishment of the users' organisation would be a further step, in addition to those which we had already taken, to secure a peaceful settlement. But, if it failed, by reason of Egyptian obstruction, he believed that we should be fully justified in having recourse to force and submitting the issue simultaneously to the Security Council.

The Lord President [Salisbury] supported the views expressed by the Lord Chancellor. In the last resort, a decision to use force could be based either on some incident in the Suez Canal or on the need to enforce respect for international obligations. He would greatly prefer that our case should be based on the second of those grounds. It was on that basis that an approach should be made, when the time came, to the Security Council. If it failed by reason of a Russian veto, it would be seen that the United Nations was incapable of enforcing the principles laid down in the preamble of the Charter. We should then be justified in taking action ourselves to enforce respect for international obligations.

The Lord Privy Seal [Butler] said that the Conservative Party in the House of Commons would be ready to support the use of force if they were satisfied that all practicable steps had been taken, without success, to secure a settlement by peaceful means.

The Prime Minister, summing up this part of the discussion, said that it was clear that the Cabinet were agreed that Egypt's disregard of her international obligations could not be tolerated and that effective international control over the Suez Canal must be re-established; that every reasonable effort must be made to secure this objective by peaceful means; but that, if these should all fail, we should be justified in the last resort in using force to restore the situation. It would be a difficult exercise of judgment to decide when the point had been reached when recourse must be had to forceful measures. In determining this, we should weigh, not only the state of public opinion in the United States, but also the views of the French, who were eager to take firm action to restore the situation and were increasingly impatient of delay.

3 October 1956

The Prime Minister said that it was difficult to forecast the course of the forthcoming discussions in the Security Council. There now seemed less reason to believe that the Egyptian Government would consider a solution on the lines which Mr Krishna Menon had canvassed during his recent visit to London, and there were no indications of the attitude which the Egyptians were likely to adopt in the Security Council. If they continued to be obdurate, world opinion might be readier to support a recourse to forceful measures. If they offered to negotiate, the task of achieving a satisfactory settlement would be more difficult and more protracted. In either event the weeks ahead would be critical; and the Government's task had not been made easier by the public statements made by Opposition leaders in this country and by members of the United States Administration.

In discussion the following points were raised:–

(*a*) The view was expressed that a solution might yet be found on the general lines suggested by Mr Krishna Menon, if means could be found for supporting a scheme of that kind by effective sanctions.

(*b*) On the other hand it was recognised that our objectives would not be fully attained if we accepted a settlement of the Suez Canal dispute which left Colonel Nasser's influence undiminished throughout the Middle East.

(*c*) There was little doubt that, among the Arab peoples of the Middle East, Colonel Nasser's prestige was increasing. And there was evidence that he was already seeking to foment discontent with the existing régimes in other Arab countries. Disturbing reports had been received of dissident movements in Libya, Saudi Arabia and Iraq.

(*d*) Among the leaders of organised labour in this country opinion was hardening against the use of force as a means of securing a settlement of the Suez dispute. If it became necessary to have recourse to force, industrial trouble must be expected, especially in the docks and in the coal mines. On the other hand, there was some evidence that among the workers themselves there was more support for the Government's policy than might be assumed from the public statements of their leaders.

18 October 1956

The Foreign Secretary [Lloyd] reported to the Cabinet the results of the discussions in the Security Council on the Suez Canal dispute.

In discussion there was general agreement that the outcome of the proceedings in the Security Council was as favourable, from our point of view, as could have been hoped. The statement of principles, which had been passed unanimously, covered the substance of the demands made by the principal users of the Canal. In particular, it was satisfactory that unanimous approval had been given to the proposition that 'the operation of the Canal should be insulated from the politics of any country.' The declaration that unresolved disputes between the Suez Canal Company and the Egyptian Government should be settled by arbitration was also of importance as tending to throw doubt on Egypt's right to nationalise the Company. The second part of the resolution, though it had been vetoed by the Soviet Union, had been supported by nine out of the eleven members of the Council. It endorsed the proposals put forward on behalf of the eighteen Powers after the first London Conference, as consistent with the principles subsequently approved by the Security Council and designed to secure a peaceful settlement of the dispute. Although it also invited the Egyptian Government to put forward alternative proposals, it asked that these should be made known promptly and that they should be not less effective than those of the eighteen Powers. It also recognised the competence of the Suez Canal Users' Association to receive dues payable by ships of its members. Finally, it was to be noted that we had contrived to avoid the appointment of any mediator or negotiating body, or the tabling of any amendment which might limit our future freedom of action.

The Cabinet agreed that, in public statements made before and after the forthcoming reassembly of Parliament, emphasis should be laid on the degree of support which we had obtained in the Security Council for the stand which we had taken in this dispute. We had taken the initiative in referring the matter to the Security Council: we should now be careful to retain that initiative. We should declare our readiness to hold further discussions with the Egyptians, within the limits of the second part of the Security Council's resolution. We should stress the fact that the Council had asked the Egyptians to put forward their proposals promptly. And, as this second part of the resolution had been vetoed, we might be well-advised to make it clear to the Egyptians by some formal communication, the terms of which would need to be agreed with the French Government, that we were awaiting their proposals.

The Cabinet—
(1) Took note of the outcome of the proceeds in the Security Council on the Suez dispute.
(2) Invited the Foreign Secretary to concert with the French Government the terms of a communication to the Egyptian Government inviting them to submit without delay their proposals for carrying into effect the principles which had been unanimously approved by the Security Council.
(3) Took note that, in a public speech which he was to make on 20th October, the Foreign Secretary would bring out the main points which had been stressed in the Cabinet's discussion.

The Cabinet then considered the general situation in the Middle East.

The Prime Minister said that, when the proceedings in the Security Council were completed, he and the Foreign Secretary had visited Paris in order to discuss with French Ministers what further steps could now be taken towards a settlement of the Suez dispute. They had taken the earliest opportunity to hold these consultations, in view of the increasing tension in the Middle East. The political situation in Jordan was unstable, and there were signs that Israel might be preparing to make some military move. If the Israelis attacked Jordan, we should be in a position of very great difficulty. Despite the terms of the Tripartite Declaration of 1950, the French had made it plain that they would not be able in those circumstances to assist Jordan; and it was evident that the United States Government would be most reluctant to intervene. We, on the other hand, had our separate obligations under the Anglo-Jordan Treaty; but it would be contrary to our interests to act, at this time and alone, in support of Jordan against Israel. Therefore, in his conversations with the French, he had proceeded on the basis that every possible effort should be made to ensure that the Israelis should not at this stage attack Jordan. If they contemplated any military operations against the Arabs, it would be far better from our point of view that they should attack Egypt; and he had reason to believe that, if they made any military move, it would be made in that direction. He had therefore thought it right to make it known to the Israelis, through the French, that in the event of hostilities between Egypt and Israel the United Kingdom Government would not come to the assistance of Egypt, because Egypt was in breach of a Security Council resolution and had repudiated Western aid under the Tripartite Declaration. He had added, in this message to the Israelis, that different considerations would apply to Jordan, to whom the United Kingdom Government had firm Treaty obligations in addition to those under the Tripartite Declaration.

The Cabinet should therefore be aware that, while we continued to seek an agreed settlement of the Suez dispute in pursuance of the resolution of the Security Council, it was possible that the issue might be brought more rapidly to a head as a result of military action by Israel against Egypt.

It was against this background that he and the Foreign Secretary had been considering, in the last few days, the proposal that troops from Iraq should be stationed in Jordan. This movement, if it had been carried out earlier, might have helped to stabilise the political situation in Jordan. The Israelis had, however, chosen to regard it as a potential threat against them, despite the assurances which they had been given to the contrary; and partly on this account and partly perhaps because of pressure from Egypt, the Jordan Government had now asked that the Iraqi troops which had been moved up to the frontier should not at this stage cross it. In view of the attitude which the Israelis had adopted towards these troop movements, we should be accepting a heavy responsibility if we now pressed the Government of Iraq or of Jordan to allow the movement to be completed. On the other hand there was a grave risk that the elections which were to be held in Jordan on 21st October might go in Egypt's favour, and in that event Jordan might pass wholly under the influence of Egypt. On balance it had seemed best that Iraqi troops should not move into Jordan at the present time.

23 October 1956 (Confidential Annex)

The Prime Minister recalled that, when the Cabinet had last discussed the Suez situation on 18th October, there had been reason to believe that the issue might be brought rapidly to a head as a result of military action by Israel against Egypt. From secret conversations which had been held in Paris with representatives of the Israeli Government, it now appeared that the Israelis would not alone launch a full-scale attack against Egypt. The United Kingdom and French Governments were thus confronted with the choice between an early military operation or a relatively prolonged negotiation. If the second course were followed, neither we nor the French could hope to maintain our military preparations in their present state of readiness – on our side some of the reservists would have to be released, some of the requisitioned merchant ships would have to be released for commercial trading and others would have to be re-loaded – and our position of negotiating from strength would to some extent be impaired. The French Government were seriously concerned at this possibility and were disposed to favour early military action. They had recently received special provocation from Egypt, through the capture of a ship conveying arms from Egypt to the rebel forces in Algeria, and they might regard this as a sufficient ground for military action against Egypt. They would not however be in a position to take such action effectively unless we gave them facilities to operate from Cyprus, and it was possible that they might press us to grant those facilities.

In discussion the Cabinet were informed that the Egyptian Government were now ready to put forward, in response to the second part of the Security Council resolution, alternative proposals for the future control of the Suez Canal. It was unlikely that these would provide all the safeguards which we thought necessary; but, in the opinion of the Secretary-General of the United Nations, they would afford a basis for renewed discussions.

The Foreign Secretary [Lloyd] said that he would not exclude the possibility that we might be able to reach, by negotiation with the Egyptians, a settlement which would give us the substance of our demand for effective international supervision of the Canal. There were, however, three serious objections to a policy of seeking a settlement by negotiation. First, it now seemed clear that the French Government would not give their full co-operation in such a policy. Secondly, it was evident that some relaxation of our military preparations would have to be made and to that extent we should weaken our negotiating position. Thirdly, he saw no prospect of reaching such a settlement as would diminish Colonel Nasser's influence throughout the Middle East.

The Prime Minister said that grave decisions would have to be taken by the Cabinet in the course of the next few days. For the present, however, the discussion could not be carried further until the attitude of the French Government was more clearly known. The French Foreign Minister had been asked to come over to London for consultations that evening; and the result of those consultations would be reported to the Cabinet on the following day.

24 October 1956 (Confidential Annex)

The Cabinet were informed of the results of the consultations which had been held with the French Foreign Minister on the previous evening. The French Government had withdrawn their Ambassador from Cairo, as a protest against Egypt's complicity in the supply of arms to the Algerian rebels, and had brought this incident to the notice of the Security Council. In these circumstances they were not anxious for an early resumption of negotiations with the Egyptians on the Suez Canal issue. On the other hand they recognised the urgent need to bring that issue to a head. They were unwilling to use the gun-running incident as a ground for taking military action against Egypt: they preferred that such action should be based on grounds which concerned the United Kingdom as well as France. While they favoured early military action they were unable to find any sufficient grounds for undertaking it at the present time.

The Cabinet were informed that the military operation which had been planned could not be held in readiness for many days longer. There was growing dis-satisfaction among the reservists who had been recalled for service, and it would be difficult to retain them for much longer unless there was some significant development in the Suez dispute by which they could be convinced that their services would soon be required. Moreover, the condition of the vehicles which had been loaded in merchant ships for many weeks was now deteriorating, and the time was fast approaching when they would have to be unloaded and serviced. For both these reasons the military authorities would prefer to adopt, after the end of October, a new military plan which could be held in readiness to be put into operation, at about fourteen days' notice, at any time throughout the winter. Under this plan the reservists would be released, and again recalled when a fresh emergency arose; and the vehicles would be unloaded from merchant ships and, for the most part, stored on land. It would be difficult to switch over to this winter plan without giving the public the impression that our military precautions were being relaxed. This could not fail to weaken our bargaining position in any negotiations which were undertaken with the Egyptian Government on the Suez Canal issue.

In discussion of the possibility of military action against Egypt the following points were raised:–

(*a*) If a military operation had to be undertaken during the winter months, it would be similar in scope to that which had been planned for the summer, and it would have the same objectives. The first objective would be to obtain control over the Suez Canal, by landing an Anglo-French force after preliminary air bombardment designed to eliminate the Egyptian Air Force and to weaken the power of resistance of the Egyptian Army. It was now known, however, that, if such an operation were launched, Israel would make a full-scale attack against Egypt; and this might have the effect of reducing the period of preliminary air bombardment. The second objective of the operation would be to secure the downfall of Colonel Nasser's regime in Egypt.

(*b*) Was it not likely that such an operation would unite the Arab world in support of Egypt? *The Prime Minister* said that this was a serious risk; but against it must be set the greater risk that, unless early action could be taken to damage Colonel Nasser's prestige, his influence would be extended throughout the Middle East to a degree which would make it much more difficult to overthrow him. It was known that he was already plotting *coups* in many of the other Arab countries; and we should never have a better pretext for intervention against him than we had now as a result of his seizure of the Suez Canal. If, however, a military operation were undertaken against Egypt, its effect in other Arab countries would be serious unless it led to the early collapse of Colonel Nasser's regime. Both for this reason, and also because of the international pressures which would develop against our continuance of the operation, it must be quick and successful.

(*c*) Military action against Egypt would presumably involve serious risks to British lives and property, both in Egypt and in other Arab countries. The Cabinet were informed that, within the limits of what was practicable, preparations had already been made to protect British civilians and the dependants of Service personnel throughout the Middle East.

The Cabinet then considered the prospects of bringing the Suez issue to a head by diplomatic means. The Egyptians might be asked to produce, within a specified time limit, their alternative proposals for placing the Canal under international supervision. This course would be in conformity with the Security Council resolution. It was, however, open to two objections. First, the French would not welcome an early resumption of the negotiations with Egypt. Secondly, if such a demand were made, the Egyptians were likely to comply with it – by producing within the specified time proposals which, though unsatisfactory, would appear to afford a basis for discussion. In that event a breaking point could only be reached after several days of discussion. If therefore the Cabinet chose the course of negotiation they would face a dilemma. They could frame their demands in such a way as to make it impossible for the Egyptians to accept them – being resolved, on an Egyptian refusal, to take military action designed to overthrow Colonel Nasser's regime. Alternatively, they could seek the sort of settlement of the Canal issue which might be reached by negotiation – recognising that, by accepting such a settlement, they would abandon their second objective of reducing Colonel Nasser's influence throughout the Middle East.

The Prime Minister, summing up the discussion, said that the choice before the Cabinet was now clear. Before their final decision was taken, further discussions with the French Government would be required.

25 October 1956

The Cabinet resumed their consideration of the Suez Canal situation.

The Prime Minister recalled that, at the time of the Cabinet's discussion on 18th October, there had been reason to believe that the issue might be brought rapidly to a head as a result of military action by Israel against Egypt. Later, on 23rd October, he had informed the Cabinet that it no longer seemed likely that Israel would alone launch a full-scale attack against Egypt. It now appeared, however, that the Israelis were, after all, advancing their military preparations with a view to making an attack on Egypt. They evidently felt that the ambitions of Colonel Nasser's Government threatened their continued existence as an independent State and that they could not afford to wait for others to curb his expansionist policies. The Cabinet must therefore consider the situation which was likely to arise if hostilities broke out between Israel and Egypt and must judge whether it would necessitate Anglo-French intervention in this area. The French Government were strongly of the view that intervention would be justified in order to limit the hostilities and that for this purpose it would be right to launch the military operation against Egypt which had already been mounted. Indeed, it was possible that if we declined to join them they would take military action alone or in conjunction with Israel. In these circumstances the Prime Minister suggested that, if Israel launched a full-scale military operation against Egypt, the Governments of the United Kingdom and France should at once call on both parties to stop hostilities and to withdraw their forces to a distance of ten miles from the Canal; and that it should at the same time be made clear that, if one or both Governments failed to undertake within twelve hours to comply with these requirements, British and French forces would intervene in order to enforce compliance. Israel might well undertake to comply with such a demand. If Egypt also complied, Colonel Nasser's prestige would be fatally undermined. If she failed to comply, there would be ample justification for Anglo-French military action against Egypt in order to safeguard the Canal. We must face the risk that we should be accused of collusion with Israel. But this charge was liable to be brought against us in any event; for it could now be assumed that, if an Anglo-French operation were undertaken against Egypt, we should be unable to prevent the Israelis from launching a parallel attack themselves; and it was preferable that we should be seen to be holding the balance between Israel and Egypt rather than appear to be accepting Israeli co-operation in an attack on Egypt alone.

The Foreign Secretary [Lloyd] supported the suggestion put forward by the Prime Minister. He believed that, unless prompt action were taken to check Colonel Nasser's ambitions, our position would be undermined throughout the Middle East. The situation in Jordan had already deteriorated seriously. In Syria we had reason to believe that there was Russian equipment sufficient for two divisions. In Libya a conspiracy against the existing régime was far advanced, with aid from Egypt. And in Iraq the Egyptians were doing all they could to undermine the authority of Nuri's Government. Our influence throughout the Middle East was gravely threatened. It was true that, from the point of view of opinion throughout the Arab States, Israel's intervention in our dispute with Egypt would be unfortunate. But there seemed to be little prospect of any other early opportunity for bringing this issue to a head.

In discussion the following arguments were advanced in support of the proposal put forward by the Prime Minister:–

(*a*) Our action would be defensible in international law; for we should be intervening to prevent interference with the free flow of traffic through the Canal, which was an international necessity. We should be entitled to use whatever force was necessary for that purpose, and the degree of force used could match the extent of the opposition encountered. The United States had acted in conformity with these principles on many occasions in the last hundred years.

(*b*) A crisis in the Middle East could not now be long delayed. Even if we decided to pursue negotiations with the Egyptians, we should still feel it necessary to maintain our military precautions in the Eastern Mediterranean, partly in order to enable us to negotiate from strength, but also in order to be ready to deal with the more widespread disorder and conflict which seemed likely to break out. If, for these reasons, force might ultimately have to be used, would it not be used more effectively and with more limited damage if we acted promptly now when an Anglo-French operation was already mounted?

On the other hand, doubts were expressed on the following grounds:–

(c) Our action would cause offence to the United States Government and might do lasting damage to Anglo-American relations. There was no prospect of securing the support or approval of the United States Government. If, however, it became necessary to launch the Anglo-French operation, they should be notified of the decision and of the reasons which had impelled us to take it.

(d) In inviting the two sides to withdraw their forces to a distance of ten miles from the Canal, we should not appear to be holding the balance evenly between Israel and Egypt. For we should be asking the Egyptians to withdraw still further within their territory, while leaving the Israel forces on Egyptian soil well in advance of their own frontier.

(e) We could be charged with failure to comply with our obligations under the Tripartite Declaration. For Egypt had not formally released us from those obligations.

(f) In seeking to separate the two belligerents we should be purporting to undertake an international function without the specific authority of the United Nations. If we followed the course proposed, our request to the two belligerents should immediately be notified to the United Nations.

After further discussion, the Cabinet – 'Agreed in principle that, in the event of an Israeli attack on Egypt, the Government should join with the French Government in calling on the two belligerents to stop hostilities and withdraw their forces to a distance of ten miles from the Canal; and should warn both belligerents that, if either or both of them failed to undertake within twelve hours to comply with these requirements, British and French forces would intervene in order to enforce compliance.'

30 October 1956

The Cabinet were informed that on the previous evening Israeli troops had crossed the frontier into Egypt and were advancing in strength towards the Suez Canal. So far they seemed to have met with little resistance from the Egyptian forces and they had made substantial progress. Their main force was reported to have reached a point half way between the frontier and the Canal, and a smaller contingent was believed to be striking south towards Suez. It seemed evident that a serious threat to the security of the Canal was developing.

The Prime Minister and the Foreign Minister of France were

expected to arrive in London later that morning, for consultations on this situation. Drafts had been prepared of notes to be addressed, on behalf of the two Governments, to the Governments of Egypt and Israel. The purpose of these notes was to call on both sides to stop hostilities and to withdraw their forces to a distance of ten miles from the Canal; and the draft note to the Egyptian Government also asked that Anglo-French forces should be allowed to move temporarily into key positions at Port Said, Ismailia and Suez in order to guarantee freedom of transit through the Canal. It was proposed that if, at the expiration of twelve hours from the delivery of these notes, one or both Governments had failed to undertake to comply with the requirements stated in them, British and French forces should intervene in order to enforce compliance.

The Cabinet approved the terms of these draft notes as a basis for the forthcoming consultation with French Ministers.

The Cabinet next considered the draft of a statement to be made that afternoon in the House of Commons by the Prime Minister. This draft was also approved, subject to certain minor amendments.

Discussion then turned on the attitude which the United States Government were likely to take towards these developments. *The Foreign Secretary* [Lloyd] said that he had been informed by the United States Ambassador in London that the United States Government were proposing to ask the Security Council to consider urgently a resolution condemning Israel as an aggressor. He had suggested to the Ambassador that such a resolution would be open to criticism on the ground that Israel was acting in self-defence; and he had emphasised the assurances which we had received that Israel did not contemplate any attack on Jordan. He was not certain, however, that the United States Government would be influenced by these arguments and it was for consideration whether, if the French Government agreed, we should attempt to persuade them to support the action which we and the French were proposing to take to bring to an end the hostilities between Israel and Egypt. As there had been little fighting so far between Israeli and Egyptian forces, it seemed possible that our action might be deferred for twenty-four hours; and in that event there would be time to make such an appeal to the United States Government.

Discussion showed that the Cabinet were in general agreement with this suggestion. Even though it was unlikely that the United States Government would respond to such an appeal, we should do our utmost to reduce the offence to American public opinion which was liable to be caused by our notes to Egypt and Israel. Our reserves of gold and dollars were still falling at a dangerously rapid rate; and, in view of the extent to which we might have to rely on American economic assistance, we could not afford to alienate the United States Government more than was absolutely necessary.

4 November 1956

The Prime Minister informed the Cabinet that the United Nations Assembly, in special emergency session, had adopted two resolutions, one put forward by Canada, the other by a group of Afro-Asian States led by India. The Canadian resolution requested the Secretary-General to submit within forty-eight hours a plan for the constitution of a United Nations force to secure and supervise the cessation of hostilities in the Suez Canal area. The Afro-Asian resolution authorised the Secretary-General to arrange an immediate cease-fire in the area within twelve hours. The Secretary-General had now transmitted this demand to the United Kingdom Government in a letter which made it clear that, as the representative of the Israel Government had offered in the debate in the United Nations Assembly to accept a cease-fire, and as Egypt had previously agreed to order a cease-fire, it now lay wholly within the capacity of the United Kingdom and French Governments to bring the hostilities in Egypt to an end. This letter placed a heavy onus of responsibility on the Governments of the United Kingdom and France; for it implied that, unless they accepted a cease-fire, they would alone be responsible for the continuance of hostilities which it had been the professed intention of their intervention to stop. If both the Israelis and the Egyptians were in fact willing to accept a cease-fire, it would be difficult to deny that the purpose of our intervention in Egypt had already been achieved.

Our reply to the Secretary-General's message would need to be despatched not later than midnight. It was therefore necessary to decide whether we should allow the initial phase of our occupation of the Canal area to proceed, as planned, in the early hours of the following morning and, if so, what reply we should send to the United Nations.

In discussion it was recognised that three courses of action were possible:—

(*i*) The initial phase of the occupation, consisting of the landing of British and French parachute troops at Port Said, should be allowed to proceed, and the United Nations should be informed that, although this action had been made imperative by the need to re-establish authority in the Suez Canal area, we remained willing to transfer the responsibility for policing that area to a United Nations force as soon as such a force could be effectively constituted and on the spot. We could not, however, accept the suggestion that this force should not include British and French detachments.

(*ii*) The parachute landings should be suspended for the next twenty-four hours in order to give the Governments of Egypt and Israel an opportunity to agree to accept a United Nations force in the Suez Canal area and to allow the United Nations time to consider whether the Anglo-French force should effect the landing already planned as an advance guard of the ultimate United Nations force.

(*iii*) We should defer further military action indefinitely, on the ground that by bringing to an end the hostilities between Egypt and Israel we had achieved the substance of our original objective, and that we must henceforward be content to exert such pressure as we could maintain through political and diplomatic channels to secure a final settlement of the problems of the Suez Canal area under the aegis of the United Nations.

It was agreed that there were serious political disadvantages in refusing to suspend military action in defiance of majority opinion in the United Nations. The Egyptian Government had already agreed to the cease-fire which the General Assembly had demanded; and the latest reports suggested that the Israeli Government had also accepted this demand. If so, it would be difficult to sustain the argument that further military action by ourselves was necessary in order to separate the combatants; and, if the initial phase of the Anglo-French landing encountered opposition and had to be reinforced by air or naval bombardment resulting in heavy civilian casualties, we might well be unable to sustain our position in the face of world opinion. We should run a grave risk that the United Nations would feel compelled to adopt collective measures, including oil sanctions, against the United Kingdom and France.

On the other hand, the dangers inherent in deferring the initial parachute landings for even a brief interval were no less great. If the momentum of the Anglo-French operation was allowed to slacken, the weight of public opinion would be against any resumption of the attack; and, since we could not rely on the early intervention of an effective United Nations force, we should fail to achieve our main purpose of establishing an impartial authority between Egypt and Israel.

The Cabinet were informed that prospects for the initial parachute landings were now more favourable than had been expected on the previous day. The Egyptian forces appeared to be withdrawing from

Port Said towards Cairo, probably in order to protect the seat of Government until a United Nations force arrived. There was now a reasonable chance that the parachute forces could be landed at Port Said and could secure a sufficient length of the port front without encountering such resistance as would make a heavy bombardment unavoidable.

After a full discussion *The Prime Minister* invited each of his colleagues to indicate his view on the three alternative courses set out above. It then became clear that the preponderant opinion in the Cabinet was in favour of the first course, viz., allowing the initial phase of the Anglo-French occupation of the Canal area to continue as planned. Two Ministers were inclined to favour the third course of deferring further military action indefinitely; but they made it clear that, if a majority of the Cabinet favoured a different course, they would support it. Four Ministers were in favour of the middle course of suspending parachute landings for twenty-four hours; but these Ministers also made it clear that, if the majority favoured a different course, they would support it. *The Paymaster-General* [Monckton] said that he remained in favour of suspending further military action indefinitely and that, if this course did not commend itself to his colleagues, he must reserve his position.

The Prime Minister, summing up the discussion, said that it was evident that the overwhelming balance of opinion in the Cabinet was in favour of allowing the initial phase of the military operation to go forward as planned. This being so, he proposed that the United Nations should be informed that it remained necessary, in the view of the Governments of the United Kingdom and France, to interpose a force between Egypt and Israel in order to prevent the continuance of hostilities, to secure the speedy withdrawal of Israeli forces, to restore traffic through the Suez Canal and to promote a settlement of the outstanding problems of the area. For this purpose certain Anglo-French operations with strictly limited objectives would continue; but, as soon as the Israeli and Egyptian Governments accepted a plan, endorsed by the United Nations, for an international force with the above functions, the United Kingdom and France would stop all military action. A new and constructive solution of the problems of the Middle East would, however, remain urgent. To this end an early meeting of the Security Council should be called, at Ministerial level, in order to work out an international settlement which would be likely to endure, together with the means to enforce it.

At the end of the Cabinet's discussion information was received that, contrary to earlier reports, the Government of Israel, while willing in principle to agree to cease hostilities in the Canal area, had now made it clear that they were not prepared to do so on the conditions specified in the United Nations Resolution. It thus appeared that a cease-fire had not yet been achieved in the area; and this, coupled with the refusal of Israel to accept a United Nations force and to withdraw from the Egyptian territory which she had occupied, was a sufficient ground for proceeding with police action in the area of the Canal. In these circumstances—

The Cabinet—

(1) Agreed that subject to the concurrence of the French Government, the initial phase of the Anglo-French occupation of the Suez Canal area should be put into effect on the lines proposed.

(2) Invited the Foreign Secretary to reply to the communication from the Secretary-General of the United Nations on the lines agreed in their discussion.

6 November 1956

The Foreign Secretary [Lloyd] said that the Secretary-General of the United Nations had asked the Governments of the United Kingdom and France whether they would recognise the decision of the General Assembly, establishing a United Nations Command, as meeting their condition for a cease-fire. He was also asking the Government of Israel if they were able to accept the resolution of the General Assembly on the establishment of a United Nations Command. If he received affirmative replies to these questions he intended to address to the four Governments a further communication calling for an agreed cease-fire.

In deciding what reply should be sent to this enquiry, the Cabinet would wish to take account of the following considerations:–

(*i*) It was now urgently necessary that we should regain the initiative in bringing hostilities to an end while there was an opportunity to carry with us the more moderate sections of opinion in the General Assembly.

(*ii*) It was equally important that we should shape our policy in such a way as to enlist the maximum sympathy and support from the United States Government.

(*iii*) But we must also maintain our position against the Soviet Union. A menacing letter had just been received from President Bulganin calling on the United Kingdom to stop the war in Egypt, and stating that the Soviet Government were submitting to the United Nations a proposal to employ, together with other members of the

United Nations, naval and air forces in order to bring the war in Egypt to an end and to curb aggression. We must not appear to be yielding in face of Soviet threats, and our reply to the Secretary-General of the United Nations must not be such as to give that impression.

In discussion the following points were made:–

(*a*) It would still be practicable to proceed with the Anglo-French occupation of the Canal area, regardless of opposition from any quarter. But, if we adopted this course, we must reckon with the possibility of a Soviet invasion of Syria or some other area in the Middle East, and possibly a direct Soviet attack on the Anglo-French forces in the Canal area. It was also probable that the other Arab States in the Middle East would come actively to the aid of Egypt, and that the United Nations would be alienated to the point of imposing collective measures, including oil sanctions, against the French and ourselves.

(*b*) If we agreed to break off hostilities at once, we could maintain that we had achieved our primary objectives. The fighting in the Canal area had been brought to an end; and the United Nations had agreed in principle that an international force should be established in that area. On the other hand, the United Nations had not accepted the definition of the functions of the international force which we had proposed; and, if its membership was to be confined to States who were not members of the Security Council, this would exclude the Anglo-French contingent which was already moving into position. There remained, therefore, a real risk that an effective international force would never be established in the Canal area; and, if we accepted a cease-fire at a moment when we had only just occupied Port Said and had not yet secured Ismailia and Suez, we should appear to have fallen short of that effective occupation of the Canal area which we had publicly declared to be one of our objectives. In addition, the Canal was now blocked to shipping; and, if we had to wait until an international force was available to remove the obstruction, free transit might not be restored for many months.

Discussion showed that there was general agreement in the Cabinet that, in order to regain the initiative and to re-establish relations with those members of the United Nations who were fundamentally in sympathy with our aims, we should agree, subject to the concurrence of the French Government, to stop further military operations provided that the Secretary-General of the United Nations could confirm that the Governments of Egypt and Israel had now accepted an unconditional cease-fire and that the international force to be set up would be competent to secure and to supervise the attainment of

the objectives set out in the operative paragraphs of the original
resolution passed by the General Assembly on 2nd November. In
addition, we should state that, pending confirmation of these assumptions, the Anglo-French force would cease fire at some point during
the day, the exact time to be determined in the light of operational
considerations. But we should at the same time emphasise that the
clearing of the Suez Canal, which was in no sense a military operation,
was now a matter of great urgency, and that we proposed that the
technicians accompanying the Anglo-French force should begin this
work at once.

The Cabinet—
Invited the Foreign Secretary, subject to the concurrence of the
French Government, to reply to the Secretary-General of the
United Nations on the lines indicated above.

Appendix III

Memorandum by the Chiefs of Staff to the Egypt Committee of the Cabinet, 8 November 1956

The Situation

1 Our forces hold Port Said and the causeway as far south as Kantara. The Egyptian forces, particularly their Air Force, have suffered a severe defeat, but Nasser is still in power supported by that considerable part of the Egyptian Army which remains intact. The war has not been brought home to the ordinary Egyptian and he has therefore had no reason to lessen his allegiance to Nasser.

2 There are no immediate military factors to prevent us from exploiting our success, but for political reasons we have accepted a cease fire. This has been forced on us by:–

    (*a*) UNO pressure.

    (*b*) The possibility of Russian intervention and the consequent necessity for realigning ourselves alongside the United States from whom our previous actions have estranged us.

    (*c*) The political climate in the United Kingdom.

3 The attitude of the other Arab States has so far been conditioned by the violence and success of the Israeli and Anglo-French operations. Whilst the Arab States are likely to retain a healthy respect for the Israelis after their overwhelming defeat of the Egyptians, and hence are unlikely to take overt unsupported action against them, the premature suspension of Anglo-French operations is likely to make it increasingly difficult for our Arab friends to hold the position unless we are also associated with action against Israel. This will be particularly true if we appear to give way before Russian pressure.

4 The possibility of setting up a UNO Force to separate the

contestants and to secure a peaceful solution is now the subject of a UNO resolution. The UNO Force covered by this resolution will be designed solely for the purpose of stopping hostilities and restoring the status quo on the frontiers. There has been no suggestion that it should in any way seek to impose a settlement of the Suez Canal dispute. Permanent Members of the Security Council will be ruled out from contributing to this force. It will, therefore, not include British or French contingents.

United Kingdom Aims

5 Her Majesty's Government have expressed the British aims for the current operation as being to separate Egyptian and Israeli forces, to ensure the security of the Suez Canal and to obtain the withdrawal of Israeli forces to the Gaza Area. Tacit aims have been to impose a satisfactory settlement of the Suez Canal dispute with Egypt and to effect the downfall of Nasser.

Likely Developments

6 It is clear that we can no longer achieve our tacit aims of securing a Suez Canal settlement satisfactory to us and of overthrowing Nasser except by renewing fighting and thus flouting the United Nations resolutions with the added danger of bringing about Russian intervention. Our avowed aims would be achieved however provided either our own forces or those of UNO could keep peace and reopen the Suez Canal. The withdrawal of Israeli forces can only be achieved by United Nations action.

7 We consider that events may now follow two possible courses. If we press on with military operations, or even if we remain in occupation of Egyptian territory without fighting, it seems likely that Russia will intervene either covertly in the shape of volunteers, or overtly as the so called agent of the United Nations. Whatever the course of events Russia is likely to re-constitute the Egyptian air force and thereby pose a serious threat to all our forces in the area.

Alternative Courses of Action

8 There are three courses of action open to us:–

    (*a*) To proceed with our original plan and occupy the Canal Zone, accepting the risks involved, with no restriction on air operations.

(*b*) To withdraw unconditionally in compliance with the United Nations resolutions.

(*c*) To remain in our present positions until we can hand over to a UNO force.

9 From the military point of view there are no immediate factors which rule out course (*a*), but if this course were politically acceptable we should presumably not already have agreed to a cease fire. We therefore do not consider this course further (but see para. 13 below).

10 In the absence of wholehearted United States support both inside and outside UNO, course (*b*) may be forced on us. It would, however, represent a major success for Russia (and Nasser) and a major defeat not only for Britain and France, but for the West, and its repercussions throughout the Middle East would be disastrous. We must therefore seek to contrive a means of avoiding this course.

11 Course (*c*) entails only slightly less risk of Russian intervention than does course (*a*), but there is a possibility that the United States could be persuaded to underwrite it as the least harmful to Western interests of the alternatives now open to us. Time is the crux of the matter, and we consider that our chances of being able to follow this course are in direct ratio to the speed with which at least a token United Nations Force can be flown in to replace our own. We do not consider that an offer to put our own forces under the United Nations Commander would be accepted by UNO.

Canal Clearance

12 The clearance of the Canal is now Her Majesty's Government's first priority in the area. Until it has been seen how UNO reacts to our proposal that Anglo-French clearance teams should undertake the task it is not possible to relate it to the three possible courses of action discussed above.

Conclusions

13 We conclude that the least damaging course to follow is course (*c*). In view of the highly inflammable situation in the Middle East and the unpredictable Russian reactions, however, we consider that we should be prepared in the worst case for a Russian sponsored war in the Middle East involving major threats to:

(*a*) Our position in Port Said;

(*b*) All sources of oil in the Middle East;

(*c*) Our Mediterranean bases.

Suez: a Chronology

This chronology is based in part on one that accompanied Peter Hennessy and Mark Laity, 'Suez – what the papers say', *Contemporary Record*, vol. 1, no. 1, spring 1987. Permission to reprint parts of it is gratefully acknowledged.

1869	Suez Canal, built by Frenchman Ferdinand de Lesseps, opens.
1875	Great Britain, at the instance of Benjamin Disraeli, purchases a major shareholding in the Canal from the Egyptian Khedive.
1882	Great Britain invades Egypt.
1922	Egypt declared by Great Britain to be an independent sovereign state but British armed forces to remain.
1936	Anthony Eden successfully negotiates an Anglo-Egyptian treaty with Egyptian nationalist politicians aspiring to achieve British troop withdrawal from Egypt by 1956.
1947	British forces withdraw from Cairo and Alexandria and henceforth are confined to the Suez Canal Zone.
1952	King Farouk overthrown in coup by army officers led by Generals Neguib and Nasser.
1954	Anglo-Egyptian Agreement for withdrawal of British forces from the Canal Zone by June 1956.
1955	(February) Eden and Nasser meet in Cairo.

1955	(September) Egyptian–Czechoslovak arms deal announced.
1956	
1 March	King Hussein of Jordan dismisses Sir John Glubb.
16 May	Egypt recognizes Communist China.
19 July	American government announces it will not finance the Aswan High Dam in Egypt.
26 July	President Nasser nationalizes the Suez Canal Company.
31 July	Dulles arrives in London for talks with Britain and France.
2 August	Government announces recall of reservists.
3 August	Britain, France and the United States announce international conference to be held in London.
10 August	Chiefs of Staff present plan 'Musketeer' to the Egypt Committee of the Cabinet.
16 August	International conference opens in London.
23 August	International conference sends Menzies mission to Cairo.
3 September	Menzies and Nasser meet.
4 September	Dulles proposes idea of a Suez Canal Users' Association (SCUA) to British Ambassador in Washington.
7 September	Chiefs of Staff change invasion plan to 'Musketeer Revise'.
10 September	Egypt Committee accepts 'Musketeer Revise'.
11 September	Cabinet endorses SCUA.
12 September	SCUA announced. Dulles undermines it at Washington press conference by saying 'we do not intend to shoot our way through.'
19 September	Second international conference opens in London.
21 September	London conference approves SCUA.
23 September	Britain and France refer dispute to UN Security Council.
26 September	Eden and Lloyd to Paris for talks.

2 October	Dulles at press conference says SCUA has 'no teeth'.
5 October	Lloyd and Pineau meet Eisenhower and Dulles. Security Council debate starts. Eden enters hospital with fever.
10 October	'Six principles' for international management of Suez Canal agreed in New York by Lloyd, Pineau and Fawzi (Egyptian Foreign Minister).
14 October	Eden at Chequers to receive French emissaries, Gazier and Challe, who outline plan for Israel to invade Egypt with Britain and France separating the combatants.
16 October	Eden and Lloyd in Paris for talks.
18 October	Eden reports Paris conversations in general terms to the Cabinet.
21 October	Meeting of inner circle ministers and officials at Chequers.
22 October	Representatives of France, Britain and Israel meet at Sèvres in Paris suburbs. Foreign Secretary Lloyd represents Britain.
23 October	Cabinet told of 'secret conversations' in Paris. Pineau visits Eden in London.
24 October	Collusion agreed and a 'record' signed by representatives of British, French and Israeli governments.
25 October	Eden tells Cabinet 'we must face the risk that we should be accused of collusion with Israel.'
29 October	Israelis attack Egypt.
30 October	British and French governments send ultimatums to Israel and Egypt instructing them to withdraw ten miles either side of the Canal to allow Anglo-French occupation. Uproar in the House of Commons. At the UN Britain and France veto American resolution calling for ceasefire and Soviet resolution calling for ceasefire and withdrawal of Israeli forces. Anglo-French task force sets sail from Malta.
31 October	Anglo-French air attacks on Egyptian airfields.

Security Council calls emergency meeting of UN General Assembly.

1 November Gaitskell denounces 'act of disastrous folly'. Commons suspended after uproar. Anglo-French planes destroy 260 Egyptian aircraft. Israelis rout Egyptians in Sinai. Widespread Commonwealth condemnation. UN General Assembly meets.

2 November General Assembly calls for ceasefire.

3 November Britain and France reply to General Assembly giving conditions for ceasefire. Israel accepts ceasefire provided Egypt does the same.

4 November Egypt blocks Suez Canal. Soviets enter Budapest. Lloyd warns Egypt Committee of American oil sanctions. Cabinet meets – 12 ministers for going on, four for postponement and three for stopping. Cabinet informed while meeting in progress that Israel has *not* accepted ceasefire.

5 November British and French paratroops land in Port Said and Port Fuad. Soviets threaten rockets on Paris and London. Israel accepts ceasefire.

6 November Anglo-French seaborne landings at Port Said. Pound critical. Macmillan telephones Washington – only a ceasefire by midnight will secure American support for an International Monetary Fund loan. Macmillan reports to Cabinet. Eden telephones Mollet and Eisenhower and announces ceasefire in Commons at 6.00 p.m. effective from midnight. Anglo-French advance stops 23 miles down the Canal from Port Said.

7 November UN General Assembly agrees UN police force for Egypt.

8 November Vote of confidence in Commons: eight Conservatives abstain.

15 November Egypt Committee told no American financial support will be forthcoming until Anglo-French withdrawal from Egypt starts.

18 November	Eden's doctors say he needs a complete rest.
23 November	The Edens fly to Jamaica.
30 November	Cabinet accepts unconditional withdrawal from Egypt inevitable.
14 December	The Edens return to London.
20 December	Eden tells Commons 'there was not fore-knowledge that Israel would attack Egypt.'
22 December	Evacuation of British troops from Canal Zone completed.

1957
9 January	Eden resigns; succeeded by Macmillan.
16 March	Israel withdraws from all areas of Egypt occupied in 1956.
20–21 March	Anglo-American friendship fully restored at meeting between Eisenhower and Macmillan in Bermuda.
24 April	Suez Canal re-opened; Egypt accepts a settlement to the Suez Canal dispute based essentially on the 'six principles' negotiated in the previous October.

Dramatis Personae

ALDRICH, WINTHROP. American Ambassador in London from 1953 to 1957.

BEN-GURION, DAVID. Prime Minister of Israel from 1955 (November) to 1963.

BRIDGES, SIR EDWARD. Permanent Secretary at the Treasury from 1945 to 1956.

BUTLER, R. A. Lord Privy Seal from 1955 (December) to 1959 and Leader of the House of Commons from 1955 (December) to 1961.

CACCIA, SIR HAROLD. British Ambassador in Washington from 1956 (November) to 1963.

CHALLE, MAURICE. A Deputy Chief of Staff of the French Air Force during the Suez Crisis.

CHURCHILL, SIR WINSTON. Prime Minister from 1940 to 1945 and from 1951 to 1955 (April).

DEAN, SIR PATRICK. Deputy Under-Secretary at the Foreign Office from 1956 to 1960.

DIXON, SIR PIERSON. Permanent British Representative to the United Nations from 1954 to 1960.

DULLES, JOHN FOSTER. US Secretary of State from 1953 to 1959.

EDEN, SIR ANTHONY (LATER EARL OF AVON). Prime Minister from April 1955 to January 1957.

EISENHOWER, DWIGHT D. American President from 1953 to 1961.

EVANS, SIR HORACE. Physician to Queen Elizabeth II, to Sir Anthony Eden and to R. A. Butler.

FAWZI, MAHMOUD. Egyptian Foreign Minister from 1952 to 1964.

GAITSKELL, HUGH. Leader of the Labour Party from 1955 (December) until 1963.

GAZIER, ALBERT. French Minister of Labour during the Suez Crisis.

GLUBB, SIR JOHN. Officer Commanding Arab Legion, Jordan, from 1939 to 1956.

HAMMARSKJÖLD, DAG. Secretary-General of the United Nations from 1953 to 1961.

HEAD, ANTONY. Secretary of State for War from 1951 to 1956 (October) and Minister of Defence from 1956 (October) to 1957 (January).

HOME, LORD (LATER SIR ALEC DOUGLAS-HOME). Commonwealth Secretary between April 1955 and 1960. He was Prime Minister from October 1963 to October 1964.

HUMPHREY, GEORGE. US Treasury Secretary from 1953 to 1957.

JEBB, SIR GLADWYN. British Ambassador in Paris from 1954 to 1960.

KEIGHTLEY, SIR CHARLES. Commander-in-Chief Middle East Land Forces from 1953 to 1957 and Allied Commander-in-Chief during the Suez Operation.

KILMUIR, THE EARL OF. Lord Chancellor from 1954 to 1962.

KIRKPATRICK, SIR IVONE. Permanent Under-Secretary at the Foreign Office from 1953 to 1957.

LENNOX-BOYD, ALAN. Colonial Secretary from 1954 to 1959.

LLOYD, SELWYN. Foreign Secretary from 1955 (December) to 1960.

LODGE, HENRY CABOT. Permanent US Representative to the United Nations from 1953 to 1960.

LOGAN, SIR DONALD. Assistant Private Secretary to Selwyn Lloyd during the Suez Crisis.

MACMILLAN, HAROLD. Foreign Secretary from April to December 1955, Chancellor of the Exchequer from December 1955 to January 1957 and Prime Minister from January 1957 to October 1963.

MAKINS, SIR ROGER. British Ambassador in Washington from 1953 to 1956 (October).

MENZIES, SIR ROBERT. Australian Prime Minister from 1939 to 1941 and from 1949 to 1966.

MOLLET, GUY. French Prime Minister from January 1956 to May 1957.

MONCKTON, SIR WALTER. Minister of Defence from December 1955 to October 1956 and Paymaster-General from October 1956 to January 1957.

MOUNTBATTEN OF BURMA, EARL. First Sea Lord from 1955 to 1959.

MURPHY, ROBERT. Deputy Under-Secretary in the US State Department from 1954 to 1959.

NASSER, GAMAL ABDEL. Egyptian Prime Minister from 1954 until 1956 (July) and President from 1956 (July) until 1970.

NEHRU, JAWAHARLAL. Indian Prime Minister from 1947 to 1964.

NURI ES-SAID. Iraqi Prime Minister on numerous occasions between 1930 and his assassination in 1958.

NUTTING, SIR ANTHONY. Minister of State at the Foreign Office from 1954 to November 1956 when he resigned in protest at the Suez Operation.

PEARSON, LESTER. Canadian Foreign Minister from 1948 to 1957.

PINEAU, CHRISTIAN. French Foreign Minister from February 1956 to June 1957.

SALISBURY, FIFTH MARQUESS OF. Leader of the House of Lords from 1951 to 1957.

SHUCKBURGH, SIR EVELYN. Principal Private Secretary to Anthony Eden from 1951 to 1954 and Assistant Under-Secretary at the Foreign Office from 1954 to 1956 (June).

STOCKWELL, SIR HUGH. Allied Commander Ground Forces in the Suez Operation.

TREVELYAN, SIR HUMPHREY. British Ambassador in Cairo from 1955 to 1956.

Further Reading

There is by now a considerable literature on the Suez Affair written from a variety of national perspectives and, indeed, in several languages. Here we shall focus only on works in English that are particularly important for an understanding of the British role.

The first substantial account of what occurred was written by Sir Anthony Eden himself in *Full Circle* (London, 1960). But, to put it mildly, the work is marred by a lack of candour. In particular, the collusion with France and Israel was totally concealed.

Hugh Thomas was the first professional historian to tackle the subject in a serious way. His *The Suez Affair* (London, 1967) was a valuable pioneering effort and was based on interviews with unnamed ministers and officials. The collusion at Sèvres was revealed and readers were told that 'there is no reason to doubt that the British Minister who went to Paris was Lloyd'.

Then Sir Anthony Nutting achieved notoriety by stating, in *No End of a Lesson: the Story of Suez* (London, 1967), on the basis of his own knowledge as a Junior Minister that Lloyd had indeed met Ben-Gurion. This work has had great and perhaps excessive influence in shaping what later writers have had to say about Suez in general and Eden's role in particular. To say the least, it is by no means the work of a dispassionate observer. Hence, though an essential source, it needs to be handled with caution.

The most detailed study to date has come from Kennett Love in *Suez: the Twice-fought War* (London, 1969). Like

Thomas's work, it was based on interviews with survivors. It remains a serious part of the literature.

The 1970s were notable for the appearance of memoirs by several Cabinet Ministers who had served under Eden. Alas, Harold Macmillan, *Riding The Storm, 1956—1959* (London, 1971) and Lord Butler, *The Art of the Possible* (London, 1971) added little to what was already known about Suez. In Macmillan's case, however, it is evident that a diary exists and we must hope that its contents concerning Suez will soon be made known. (An 'authorized' biography is being prepared by Alastair Horne.) More rewarding was Selwyn Lloyd's *Suez 1956: a Personal Account* (London, 1978). He based his work on certain official records (including Cabinet Minutes) made available to him as a former Foreign Secretary and was admirably candid in confirming that he had indeed met Ben-Gurion at Sèvres. His account, moreover, raised some question marks about the reliability of the Nutting version of events throughout 1956.

In my own *Anthony Eden: a Biography* (London, 1981) I was able to present new material available in the United States, particularly at the Eisenhower Library. There was some press coverage given to revelations that the Eisenhower Administration had engaged in secret discussions with Butler, Macmillan and Salisbury without the knowledge of Eden and Lloyd during the period after the ceasefire.

A further biography (of the 'authorized' variety) was Robert Rhodes James's *Anthony Eden* (London, 1986). The author had access to material then closed under the 30-year rule. But the precise extent of what he saw has not been made clear.

Within months of the publication of Rhodes James's work the Suez archives in the Public Record Office at Kew were opened. They were more extensive than generally expected. The first book which drew on what had become available was Richard Lamb's *The Failure of the Eden Government* (London, 1987). It revealed signs of hasty composition, but contained much detail not previously known.

Four further books merit mention. One is Evelyn Shuckburgh, *Descent to Suez: Diaries 1951—56* (London, 1986). While shedding little light on the Suez Operation itself – the author was no longer near the centre of events – it is a vital source for background information. Secondly, for a view of the Suez Crisis through the eyes of Eden's Press Secretary, there is chapter 6 of William Clark, *From Three Worlds: Memoirs* (London, 1986) based in part on his contemporary diary. A third work is Roy Fullick and Geoffrey Powell, *Suez: the Double War* (London, 1979). This is the best work so far on the military aspect of the Suez Operation. Finally, on the domestic impact, there is Leon D. Epstein, *British Politics in the Suez Crisis* (London, 1964).

Many more books on Suez may be expected following the opening of the British archives for 1956. Among those said to be in preparation are large-scale analyses by Keith Kyle of Chatham House and Professor William Roger Louis of the University of Texas. Readers wishing to keep abreast of latest revelations on the matter of Suez will also be likely to profit from subscribing to *Contemporary Record*, the quarterly journal of the Institute of Contemporary British History.

Index